Qantas By G

Qantas By George!

The remarkable story of George Roberts

Paul Byrnes

The Watermark Press

First published in 2000 by
The Watermark Press,
Sydney, Australia

Reprinted 2000

National Library of Australia
Cataloguing-in-Publication data

       Byrnes, Paul.
       Qantas By George

       Includes index.
       ISBN 0 949284 52 1.

       1. Roberts, George, 1909- . 2. Aeronautical engineers -
       Australia - Biography. I. Title.

       629.13092

Designed by Suzy King
Printed in Australia by Griffin Press

CONTENTS

George Roberts on his 90th birthday.

Foreword

This book has been published as part of the proud celebration of the 80th anniversary of Qantas Airways. As the title indicates, it is the story of Qantas from the perspective of a remarkable former employee whose whole life has been interwoven with engineering, with aircraft and with Qantas.

George Roberts joined Qantas on Monday 1 November 1936. He worked as an engineer with the company for 34 years and, as this book illustrates, contributed to the reputation for engineering excellence and innovation in aviation that has been a hallmark of Qantas throughout its long and illustrious history.

Although he formally retired in 1970, he has never really left Qantas. He has continued to make an outstanding contribution to the Qantas Historical Collection and this book is a tribute to his dedication to the company, his sense of history and his foresight in keeping such a magnificent collection of photos, artefacts and memorabilia.

Qantas owes its reputation as an Australian icon to the work of thousands of employees throughout its history who have made the company what it is.

While it is not possible to pay tribute to all of them individually, this book celebrates their contribution in making Qantas the Spirit of Australia.

James Strong

Chief Executive Officer and Managing Director

Introduction

George Roberts and Australian aviation grew up together. He was born in Ipswich, Queensland in 1909, in the horse and buggy era. Six months later, John R. Duigan made the first flight in an Australian-designed and built aircraft near Kyneton, Victoria. George and his elder brother Norm took their first flight in 1920, in a flying boat on Moreton Bay. George was ten, his brother 11. A few years later they built their first glider and flew it off the roof while their parents were out. Norm piloted and George threw a mattress under him as he crashed.

They were flying even before Qantas was formed in western Queensland in November 1920. Both men would spend most of their working lives with the airline. Norm died in 1991, aged 83. At 90 George is now the oldest living former employee and the only one from the old Queensland days, before Qantas moved to Sydney.

His life has been both fortunate and adventurous, spanning two centuries and the whole modern history of trains, planes and automobiles. His father once built the former; George and his brother spent much of their early lives building, racing and sometimes crashing both the latter. They were hotrodders before the term existed, souping up Model T Fords and speed-trialling them on Southport Beach before it was the Gold Coast (they got one up to 104 mph in 1934). They built planes too, like the tiny Flying Flea, using plans published in *Newnes Practical Mechanics* magazine.

Their Flea, which really did fly, now hangs in the Queensland Museum. They were there when Charles Kingsford Smith arrived in Brisbane in 1928, the first man to fly across the Pacific. When Amy Johnson overturned on landing after an extraordinary solo flight from England, George and a friend pulled her out of her upturned Gipsy Moth, in a corn field near Eagle Farm aerodrome.

Both brothers were gifted engineers before joining the airline, but in Qantas hangars from Perth to Surabaya and Rose Bay, they found the biggest toolshed a kid could ever want and a home for their inventive and creative minds.

This book tries to illuminate their contributions. Many of the stories have never been told, nor many of the photographs published.

My warmest thanks go to Bernard Shirley, whose idea it was and who provided much encouragement. I am also indebted to the writers of various memoirs and Qantas histories, particularly John Gunn, E. Bennett-Bremner, Bruce Leonard and John Fysh for permission to quote from his father's memoirs.

Most of all, my thanks go to the remarkable George Roberts and his friend Marie. It has been a pleasure to research and write George's story. His candour, larrikin humour, extraordinary memory and acute sense of history have made the experience endlessly enjoyable. His patience with someone who couldn't tell a gasket from a gyroscope has been heroic.

This book is about him, but also for him.

Paul Byrnes
September, 2000.

Dressed to impress in February 1911: George is 14 months old, in the arms of nanny Alice Dyer, with Norm in front and Prinnie the dog behind.

CHAPTER ONE
That's my Boys

The day was warm and cloudless, perfect for flying.

The Roberts family was on holiday at Sandgate, on the shores of Moreton Bay, just east of Brisbane. It was early 1920, possibly the Easter break, about 18 months after the Great War had ended. George Roberts, aged 10, was on the water's edge with his sister Ivy and his brothers Norman and John (except everyone called him Don, because little Ivy hadn't been able to say John properly). When they heard an aeroplane engine droning out in the bay, there was great excitement, though it was not the first plane the older children had seen.

The Curtiss Seagull, with engine running, gets a push at Sandgate in early 1920.
Left to right, Norm (at bow), Ivy, unknown, Don (at wing) and George at the tail.
A few minutes later George and Norm took their first flight.

George: "I can recall that a plane flew into Ipswich before this and landed in Cribb's paddock, about a quarter of a mile from our house. It must have been just after the war. Norm and I ran from home to have a look. That was quite natural; everyone ran to have a look at an aeroplane in those days."

The plane they watched now was quite different. It was a Curtiss Seagull, an elegant flying boat built in America by Glen Curtiss. George believes this was one of two Seagulls owned by Lebbeus Hordern, of the famous Sydney department store family, who was rich and loved aeroplanes. Hordern imported the planes in February 1920. One was sent on a trip to Tasmania; George believes this was other one. There were three men in the cockpit but George does not remember who the pilot was. He was too busy gawking at the beautiful mahogany-hulled biplane.

"We watched it alight on the water and become stuck on a sandbank, quite near us. The engine was going, they couldn't move the aircraft, and we kids were in the water at the time. Norm waded out and took the bow of the aircraft, my sister took one wing and I took the other wing and we rocked the hull and got it into a deeper trough of water. The result was they were able to take off. They went off flying and came back again after half an hour and by this time the tide had risen a little and two men got out of it, and the pilot said to my father, 'what about you two kids having a flight'."

Bert Roberts had been photographing the whole adventure from the beach. Now he watched, presumably with some trepidation, as his two elder boys clambered into the open cockpit of a flimsy, new-fangled aeroplane made from wood, wire and canvas. Sitting on a wooden bench beside the pilot, they took off across the bay. There were no seatbelts, no flying goggles and no hats for the boys. George remembers spray coming over the bow as they ripped across the water, then the plane was up and his perspective on the world changed forever.

He was astonished by what he saw below. For the first time, he could see the underwater sandbanks in the bay and the long jetty jutting out from Sandgate. Off to the east was Stradbroke Island, where they had been many times on the ferry, the *Doomba*, which was now crossing the bay, a few hundred feet below them. They could see their younger brother and sister on the beach—and probably their mother, who wasn't there when the plane arrived.

"We could see out of the plane quite well, there was a windscreen in front of us. Naturally, we were tickled pink by this. We were absolutely elated by this."

As exciting as the flight was, the thing that stuck in his 10-year-old mind was the aircraft itself. "I certainly recall all the details of the aeroplane—that it was a biplane, and the stabilisers that were up on the top wing, and the pusher propeller and also that it was a six-cylinder in-line engine."

This interest in the technical detail is not as strange as it sounds. Engines and transport were the Roberts family passion, as well as their livelihood. Their father opened Roberts Motors in Ipswich in 1908, selling Ford, Fiat and Mitchell cars. He was the first in their street to own a motorcar, a Ford Model K, bought in 1908. George had learned to drive by the age of seven, though he and Norm both had trouble reaching the foot pedals.

The car dealership was at the corner of Brisbane and Gordon Streets, Ipswich, beside the coachworks begun by their grandfather Albert Edward Roberts early in the 1880s. He had been a master coachbuilder in Birmingham, Manchester and London before migrating to Australia in 1880. He must have been a good one too, because one of the last jobs he did before leaving was the full reconditioning of the gold leaf on the ceremonial coach used by the Royal family. George remembers seeing the paper patterns his grandfather traced to refurbish the gold leaf, hanging in his coachworks office in Ipswich—a fact he confirmed in 1984 on a visit to Buckingham Palace.

"I was in London as the Australian delegate to FIVA, the Federation Internationale des Vehicles Anciennes, and all of the delegates were invited to dinner at Buckingham Palace, where we met Prince Philip. After dinner, we were taken into the mews and shown through all the horse-drawn vehicles there until we reached the gold coach and I asked Prince Philip, 'do you mind if I sit in the gold coach?' He said 'why would you want to do that?' I said, 'it's my belief that the last thing that my grandfather did before leaving London was to re-gild the gold coach'. He asked me if I had anything to prove that and I said no, the proof

Top: George drew this advertising artwork for the
family business when he was about 15.
Bottom: Roberts Motors, in 1925. George stands at far
right, behind a new 1925 Essex Six and three Model T Fords.
Right: Bert Roberts. Self-portrait in the library at home.

is gone today unfortunately, but that when I first joined my grandfather in the coachbuilding business these paper patterns were on the wall of his office. They were since destroyed in a flood. 'Oh', he said, 'I will call up the curator'. The curator asked me, 'what was your grandfather's name?' I said 'Albert Edward Roberts', so he looked it up. He said, when would that have been? I said, '1878 to 1880' and he said 'yes, here it is, Albert Edward Roberts', so Prince Philip turned to me and he said, 'I think you'd better sit in the gold coach'."

Bert Roberts built the family home at 7 York Street, East Ipswich, in 1907. It had a workshop big enough for three cars and he subscribed to *Popular*

Mechanics, which the boys devoured for its detailed plans of how to build things. "If we wanted to build something, we built it," George says now.

"One thing we involved our sister in, we built a flying fox from a silky oak tree down to a rather large post that supported a grapevine trellis. We used clothesline wire for the cable and we took the front wheel off a tricycle, took the rubber tyre off the rim, and took the front forks and put them over the cable and hung it on the wheel. We considered that our sister, being by far the lightest of the three of us, should be the initial pilot. So she came up in the tree with us and took the handlebars and away she went down the wire. But we realised she was going to hit the post at the bottom. In those days, you always had an ash pit from the fireplace in the kitchen, and so we shook the wire and Ivy fell off into the ash pit. There were no injuries of course.

"We were always building something or other; we tried very much as small fellows to invent propulsion of any type. When we were in our teens, we built a small engine to work the machinery in our workshop, because there was no electricity there. There was gas, but we decided we would do it with a belt drive. It operated our grinding wheels, our drill and things."

They also built their own boat to use at Sandgate.

"We decided we should make a boat to use there and the boat had to be collapsible, otherwise it could not go on the vehicle. Vehicles of course in those days had their long running boards, plenty of room between the front mudguards and the bonnet, so we got a wide piece of timber, shaped the nose on it and then went to our mulberry tree, because the mulberry branch was

The family at Sandgate, Moreton bay in early 1920.

long, slender and very very tough and it bent easily. We pulled a number of these down, made attachments for them to this timber, which was demountable and then pulled all the top points of them together in the form of the sides of a boat. From the coachworks, we found an old canvas and put that over the top of it and attached it around. We wanted to know that it was satisfactory before going to the seaside, so we dug a hole in the backyard, filled it with water and it floated. We took it to the seaside and it worked satisfactorily."

Bert Roberts subscribed to several other British periodicals, such as *The Illustrated London News, The Strand, The Sphere, Black and White, Work* and *The Illustrated War News*. In these, Norm and George pored over the designs of the planes being flown in France and the Sinai desert by the Royal Flying Corps and the

Australian Flying Corps. The future founders of Qantas were among them, but also their own cousin, Reg Andrews.

George: "Reg inspired us very much about planes and I feel sure that he was the inspiration really of some of our interest in aircraft. He had been a fighter pilot in World War I, flying SE5A fighters. He had engine trouble and had landed between allied and enemy lines. He jumped out of his aircraft and into a shell hole for protection, but the shell hole was full of mustard gas. The result was he was sent back home in 1917 and he died in 1924, but not before he had talked very considerably to Norm and me about his flying days.

"He gave Norm a nice copy of a publication he brought back from Europe, which we have today. It's a coloured one, detailing aircraft flying in World War I. He gave us each a section of his propeller, which had been broken. He gave me his flying helmet and his goggles and I have those today. We had a lot of discussions with him. He was a sick man and he went to live on Tambourine Mountain to try and overcome the effects, because it was a little higher, better air. He lived there for quite a while and we visited him quite a lot as youths. I have no recollection of his fighting attributes at all, whether he shot down the enemy, but he must have done, to be flying SE5As. That was the best aircraft that the allies had at the time. We talked quite a lot about the flying conditions, where they were, flying over the lines and looking for the enemy, about the aeroplane itself, how he had started his training in a BE2a and how he went from there to an Avro 504K and then to a Sopwith Pup and a Sopwith Camel, before flying the SE5A."

Souvenirs of war: Reg Andrews' leather flying helmet, flying goggles and sections of his SE5A propeller.

A tradition of excellence: buggies made by George's grandfather, Ipswich, 1896.

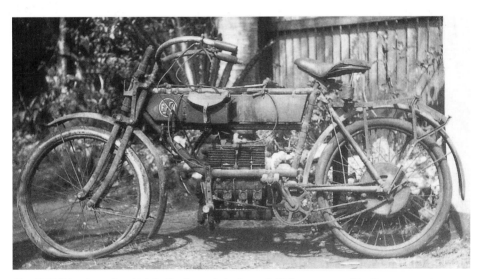

*The 1909 FN motorcycle which Dr Dunlop rode to George's birth, now owned by George.
It has four cylinders and a fixed shaft drive, but no clutch or gearbox.*

The boys drew pictures of these planes, one of which George still has: a watercolour of an Avro 504K, painted by Norm when he was about 12, with the words—The Avro in charge of Captain Roberts—in red ink beneath. (This aircraft, an allied mainstay in WWI before the introduction of the Bristol Fighter, would also become the first aircraft ordered by the newly formed Queensland and Northern Territory Aerial Services Ltd in 1920).

Curiosity was encouraged in the Roberts family home. Bert Roberts had many enthusiasms: steam engines, geology, athletics, snakes, spiders, Australian flora, gardening, music and photography. He was a gifted organist and music would often fill the house on a Sunday night. The children could all sing and George played the mouth organ, but he was an exceptional boy soprano. Between 1919 and 1921, he appeared in two J.C. Williamson Christmas pantomimes, in Brisbane and Ipswich, as a featured soloist.

Florence Roberts, their mother, known as Flo, was a gifted amateur painter and maker of handicrafts and all her children could paint and draw. She loved reading too, but had little time to indulge in it. Keeping house was arduous physical work. "There were no washing machines, no gas ovens and the heating and cooking fires had to be maintained all day."

She and George were very close, perhaps because she nearly lost him at birth and then again at age seven. George was born prematurely, at home, on December 27, 1909. He weighed only two pounds (900 grams).

"It was summertime and to make what we might call a humidicrib, they used two house bricks wrapped in cotton wool, which were placed alongside me in the cot, because of my early birth. The bricks were to keep the warmth up to the body and they were heated up in a wood stove in the kitchen, wrapped in cotton wool and placed either side of me. The doctor who came to deliver me came on a motorcycle and that motorcycle I have today. The doctor

The three sisters Field: Jessie, Florence (George's mother) and Marie, taken around 1906, before Florence married Bert Roberts.

Acting the goat: Norm drives the billy cart with George and Ivy along for the ride. George was about seven.

sold it two or three years later to an uncle of mine who lived about five doors down the street from us, and when I was five or six years of age, I was always down with my uncle, Stanley Pearce, cleaning his motorcycle. When I was about nine, he decided to move to Sydney and became the chief electrical draughtsman of Cockatoo Dock and he left the motorcycle with me and that's why I have it today. It's a four cylinder F.N., which means Fabrique Nationale, and it has no gearbox and no clutch. It's completely fixed shaft drive, but it still exists in its original state."

At age seven, George cut his foot and got blood poisoning.

"There was no such thing as penicillin, of course. I had an operation at Ipswich General Hospital on my groin to prevent it spreading, and I came through that okay."

Despite these scrapes, Flo Roberts encouraged the children to be adventurous, more so than did their father. "My mother liked her boys to be boys," George says now.

No. 7 York Street, East Ipswich, with the 13 step leap. George was named after his father's cousin, shown here at right, with George, Norm, and their father Bert.

They were certainly that. They tore around the neighbourhood on penny-farthing bikes, which were notorious for tipping their riders off head first; they ripped old prams apart to get wheels for their billy-carts. Sometimes they hitched a pair of pet billy goats to the billy-cart, with a special harness made by Goldby's Saddlery in Ipswich. They even erected square sails made from bed sheets on these carts and invented an early kind of road-sailing.

They strung a wire between two mango trees and learned how to walk a tightrope. Later, when they started souping up old Fords, they would often race each other home along York Street, bumping wheels as they vied to be first through the gates.

"My mother would just look at us and say, 'well, that's my boys'."

The house was on a large block, 107 metres deep, with a circular driveway and two impressive sets of gates; a sign that the new motor business was prospering. It was a typical 'Queenslander', built on stilts to stay above the heat, moisture and insects. All around the house was a lush garden full of Australian native flora that Bert Roberts laid out before building the home. There were five large mango trees that the boys would climb in summer after school, sitting in the boughs and gorging themselves on the fruit. There were loquats, bananas, paw paw, Brazilian cherries, delicious cherry guavas, oranges and lemons, custard apples and pomegranates, most of which went into their mother's jams and preserves. The front and back were dominated by tall Cotton and Elegant palms, 48 in all, plus a jacaranda, a poinciana and a weeping fig tree. As a child, George could put his fingers around the trunk of the fig tree. When the home was finally sold in 1995, the trunk's circumference was 7.3 metres. Behind the house was a large vegetable garden and fowl house. Like most of their neighbours, the Roberts family was fairly self-sufficient in eggs, fruit and vegetables. Men in horse-drawn carts usually delivered what they didn't have, such as bread, milk, ice and meat. Their grandfather, of course, had built most of these carts.

On the eastern side of the house, Bert Roberts built a lush fernery. "It was a very beautiful spot to be, particularly in the summers of Ipswich, which can be exceptionally hot. In our early childhood, probably up to the age of nine, we had a pet carpet snake and that snake lived there. We had no fear of it, it had no fear of us and we played with it. My father was interested in snakes and any time we went into the country and there was some snake that he had not seen previously, he would catch the snake, always by the tail, spinning it by the tail to stop it climbing up.

Wartime solidarity: The Roberts family dressed in French costumes and draped the Model T in tricolors and wattle for a procession through Ipswich. Norm, Ivy, George in front, Don in the car, and their father making a homely nurse.

"There was a toolbox on the running board of the car. He would drop the snake into that and drop the lid and put the lock on and bring it home. And then he would open the lid and allow the snake to come out, once again catch it and put it into a bottle with formalin. So we had a menagerie there of snakes in bottles. We knew our snakes very well and they didn't bother us. It was no concern at all, the same with spiders. We had trapdoor spiders, quite a lot of them, in our back paddock and we used to tease them with a straw of grass, rubbing it around the top until the trapdoor would open and the spider would grab the piece of grass and try to pull it into his nest."

There was a specimen case in the house, which the children filled with treasures: snakes, spiders, various exotic Queensland insects, a bird's nest and fossilised beetles, fish and ferns found on Denmark Hill, the highest spot in Ipswich. There were precious stones too, sapphires which they had scooped from streams in the nearby McPherson ranges, where they went exploring, at first with their father, then on their own.

George: "We knew this range backwards, particularly our sister. Ivy could go into those mountains and easily find her way out again, no problem. We had climbed most of the mountains there."

Bert Roberts would often drive the children up the steep incline of Spicer's Gap, a gradient of one in three, to spend the weekend bush walking and fossicking. On the steepest section of the road, the car would go up in reverse.

George: "There were three reasons for going up there in reverse. One is that it is the lowest ratio, the second was that the fuel flowed through to the carburettor, being gravity fed, and the third one was that if the engine stalled, you could come down frontwards, not backwards. Coming down the mountain, we always cut a tree down, attached it to the back of the car and towed the tree down the hill. That was a means of braking. It wasn't a big tree, but just enough to restrict the car. You tied the tree to the car, not by its trunk but by the top of the tree, so that branches dug in as you pulled it down the hill. That was in my father's Model T."

In the early 1920s, as the boys became more and more interested in aircraft, their father built a very large open verandah on the back of the house. Here they began construction of their first flying machine, when George was about 14.

"Our first one was a glider. The structure of that one came from *Popular Mechanics*, but it was not a very satisfactory one. It was, in the term used today, a hang-glider and on a Saturday afternoon, my father and mother always took the younger children out for a drive, leaving Norm and I at home. So one Saturday afternoon, we got this glider up to the roof of the house. Norm being the elder, got up on the peak of the house and he was going to run down and jump off the back of the house with this glider. I thought he could be injured when this happens, so the best thing I can do is get a mattress. So I got a single bed mattress and as he jumped, I threw the mattress underneath him.

"There were no injuries, but I can assure you, it was not a successful flight. It was a disaster, really, but it was the first try. The glider's wingspread was maybe 18 feet (5.5m), something like that. We were quite aware of why it didn't work. Our wing design was quite irregular, but it was according to plan as far as *Popular Mechanics* was concerned. It was very obvious that whoever drew up the plan knew very little about it either, even less than we did."

Hudson Fysh (right) in front of a Bristol fighter in Palestine. The pilot is Major S.W. Addison.

CHAPTER TWO

Boys into Men

The Great War sent many young Australian men home broken, like Reg Andrews, crippled by mustard gas. Others came home stronger, more confident and with a restless desire to do something. They had survived a war of unprecedented proportions; at the same time, they had glimpsed a wider world, as few young Australian men before them had. They had learned new skills too—like how to fly.

Returning quietly to the family farm or a job as a Tasmanian wool classer was always going to be hard for some. At least to some extent, the origins of Qantas lie in this desire for a life less ordinary.

Paul McGinness was already thinking of a career in aviation before he had learned to fly. He wrote to his mother in October 1916, from the Middle East, setting out his reasons for requesting a transfer to the Australian Flying Corps. First of these was that he was too young (at 20) to expect a commission in the 8th Light Horse Regiment, which he had joined on September 17, 1914—six weeks after war broke out. (Misspellings are as in the original letter.)

"Now in the flying core you can get a commission at 21, and with a DCM to my creddit I ought to have a good chance.

"Now another reason is aviation is only in its child-hood and say if a man had a good deal of experience in it here after the war he might follow it up in Australia, if not in the military, perhaps as a proffesion."

The youngest son of a large family, he had been born in 1896 and raised on a farm at Framlingham, near Warrnambool in Victoria. Joining a horse regiment was a natural choice, but horses were not required for the landing at Gallipoli. McGinness spent about seven months there, but he did not win the Distinguished Conduct Medal in action at Pope's Hill, as some accounts have stated. That came in the Sinai, on 13 April 1916 where he was cited for "good scouting and leadership of his troops in action" at Jif Jaffa. On Gallipoli, he was wounded slightly at Walker's Ridge, when a machine gun bullet "struck his bandolier and ploughed a red line from hip to hip". Thus wrote the *Warrnambool Standard* of April 16, 1919, in a report on McGinness's homecoming, for which he (or his letters to his family) is the most likely source. The newspaper said he was the only survivor of 150 men who went over the top at 3 a.m. on August 7. "He fell into a slight hollow right under the Turkish

Young men with a future: Hudson Fysh (left) and Paul McGinness.
Fysh sent (below) this Australian Flying Corps postcard from Palestine in November 1917.

machine guns and lay there all through that dreadful day, under the burning sun, not daring to move until dark. Then he crept back to his own trenches, but in doing so he was nearly shot by the few of his comrades who had survived out

of the second division, and who thought he was a Turk. Next morning, he went out with five volunteers to recover the body of Major Redford (his C.O.). They sapped out to within a few feet of where he lay. Four of the six went up with Sgt McQuinness [sic], but before they got back to the sap, the four were killed and Sgt McGinness had to pass the

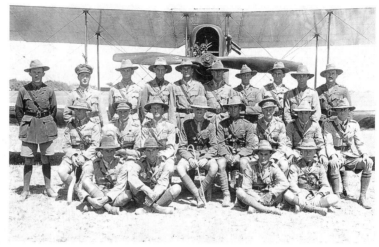

No. 1 Squadron, AFC, in Palestine, in front of a Martinsyde.
Fysh is sixth from left in the back row.

body down to one who remained in the sap. He wrote that the bullets rained round them like hailstones, but he was unscathed."

Hudson Fysh was at Gallipoli for seven months too, but it is unlikely they ever met. Fysh joined the 3rd Light Horse Regiment on August 26, 1914. He was 19. They landed at Gallipoli two weeks after the April 25 assault; McGinness was in the 8th LHR.

Fysh and McGinness were so different, it's a wonder they ever became friends. McGinness was a tearaway, or as Sir Hudson Fysh later put it "always essentially an adventurous spirit". Fysh was shy and lacking in self-confidence, at least before he went to war.

Born in 1895, he was from Launceston in Tasmania and something of a blueblood. His grand uncle Sir Philip Fysh had been premier of Tasmania at Federation in 1901, but his father's career running a softgoods business in Launceston had failed. Worse, his father's marriage to Mary Reed, from a well-to-do Launceston family, also failed.

Three children stayed with their mother; Hudson and his brother Frith were sent to live with their father on a nearby dairy farm. In *Qantas Rising*, Sir Hudson Fysh's account of the airline's early years, he writes that he ran away several times during the next year, returning to his mother until a judge allowed him to stay with her.

He was educated at Geelong Grammar, then as now an exclusive outpost of English schooling traditions, where he did well at sports, if not study. "I left Geelong, having passed just nothing, not even the Junior Public, but I have always felt that my stay there was of infinite benefit," he wrote. "It helped me gain a little confidence in myself and gave me health and friends for later life."

War gave him a lot more confidence. He discovered to his surprise that he could be brave when necessary, though his account of Gallipoli is notably un-selfserving. "For me, Gallipoli was a lesson in living, it provided a contrast with ordinary life and when looked back on at times when I've been inclined to grumble has produced the feeling that all is luxury compared to that seven months. I made no particular friends, though the basis of many friendships was formed. I lost no friends. I committed no brave deeds and gave no distinguished service. I had failed in my application for a commission with the British infantry in France, but had got a transfer to the machine guns. After all, Gallipoli was an experience: essentially a terrific personal experience."

After the evacuation from Gallipoli in December, both men were repatriated to Egypt, reunited with their horses and sent out into the Sinai desert to fight the Turks again. Fysh's Lieutenant was Ross Smith, who would soon transfer to the No. 67 Squadron, Royal Flying Corps (which became No.1 Squadron, Australian Flying Corps), and become one of the most successful pilots of the war in the Middle East. Hudson Fysh took his place as Lieutenant, then followed him into the AFC on July 6, 1917, but as an observer rather than a pilot.

There was much competition to join the Flying Corps, and transferring was not easy. Fysh had to get the consent of his own commanding officer, then be accepted by Major Richard Williams, C.O. of the No. 1 Squadron, AFC. In 1914, Williams had been the first graduate of the Central Flying School set up a year earlier at Point Cook in Victoria. He would go on to become the first Chief of Air Staff in the newly formed Royal Australian Air Force after the war, reaching the rank of Air Marshal. Later Sir Richard Williams, he became Director-General of Civil Aviation from 1946 to 1955, a job with a great deal of influence over Qantas's operations. When Lieutenant Fysh turned up at his tent at Belah in 1917, neither could have guessed how far their lives were about to become linked.

Arthur Baird was already in the AFC before McGinness and Fysh arrived. He had learned to fly in Australia before either of them, becoming an instructor at the Central Flying School, but he was also an automotive engineer, and that's where his talents were deployed once he got to Egypt in the middle of 1916. He was born in Benalla, Victoria in 1889, so he was older than Fysh and McGinness, by six and seven years. When the three came together in No. 1 Squadron, most of the seeds from which Qantas would sprout were now in place.

McGinness was the last of the three to join the AFC. He attended flying school in August 1917, but he did not reach No. 1 Squadron until March 1918. He established himself quickly as one of the best pilots.

Baird was already renowned for his ability to keep the allies' frail and outdated planes flying against superior German machines. In 1954, after Baird's death, Sir Hudson Fysh wrote: "As flight sergeant in B Flight, No. 1 Squadron, he won a decoration and the admiration of all. His ingenuity with a difficult aero engine often meant that he had much responsibility thrust upon him and I

Arthur Baird in a de Havilland Fox Moth. He learned to fly before Fysh and McGinness, but spent most of his war on the ground, fixing aircraft.

Illustrated aerial fighting in WWI, from Flying Colours, *by Captain R.H.M.S Saundby, the book Reg Andrews gave Norm in 1921. A German Albatros Scout (left), and a Martinsyde attacking a German fighter, possibly an Aviatik.*

remember at Ramleh, Palestine, in 1917, when No. 111 and 114 Squadrons were in dire trouble with their engines, he carried them through a very difficult time, and by his work on the fractious Vipers got our friends' SE5s in the air again."

Baird would gain experience on many different aircraft during the war, including the Avro 504K, the BE2e and the Bristol Fighter. Each of these would be flown in adverse conditions in western Queensland within a few years by the newly formed airline.

The aerial war in Palestine was both highly civilised and highly dangerous. The main work in No. 1 Squadron was reconnaissance, but dogfights were frequent. When the Germans shot down an opponent behind their lines, they would often fly over the next day and drop a letter, informing the Australians of the fate of their comrades. Both sides buried the other's dead with full military honours; if a man were captured, the Australians would sometimes receive a request to fly over and drop his kit on the German landing strip, which they did.

Even without the enemy, the flying was dangerous. Fysh had his first crash soon after joining, when a BE2e overladen with propaganda leaflets for the Turks stalled at about 50 feet (15m). "We picked ourselves out of the wreckage unhurt."

Choosing the right pilot to fly with was crucial and Fysh flew with 'Ginty' McGinness whenever he could. "He was a superb pilot, full of dash and adventure," Fysh wrote. "In his seven definitely confirmed victories in the air, he was hit only once, when a bullet went through the tail."

Fysh describes their first dogfight together, in which they and an escort plane took on four German Albatros two-seaters over El Afule. "I remember in the melee firing a long burst at a two-seater as it flashed past, but with no visible result. Then McGinness, making a sharp wheeling manoeuvre, was on his tail and diving fast, his front gun flat out to keep the German rear-

A young Arthur Baird working on an engine.

gunner quiet. A few close shots zipped past, the Albatros careered up in a great towering loop with McGinness now on its tail close behind. Up and up we went in an eyeball and guts-flattening manoeuvre with the ground careering away, stripping off at 200 mph with the blue sky dizzily taking its place as we reached the upside-down position.

"Ginty shot the two-seater down at the top of its loop with us also in the inverted position, the enemy then plummeting straight into the ground to end up a heap of smoking debris."

On August 31, 1918, while based at Ramleh, near Jaffa, Fysh and McGinness shot down two more German planes. The next day, they had the "not too happy, indeed sobering experience, of attending the funeral of the two German officers shot down in our lines."

Major Williams had promised Fysh that he could train as a pilot after an unspecified tour of duty as an observer, but his several requests for a transfer to the flying school at Aboukir in Egypt were unsuccessful, largely because Williams found it easier to replace pilots than observers. Fysh was not to get his chance until just before the war ended.

The training plane was an Avro 504K, with an 80-horsepower French engine, the same plane that George and Norm Roberts were reading about (and drawing pictures of) at home in Ipswich. The trainees did about 10 hours of dual flying before their first solo. "There is nothing quite like your first solo," Fysh wrote later, "up in the air alone with a feeling of being free as the air and one of the chosen few".

There was nothing quite like the second solo either in his case, because he crashed. "I suspect that I choked my engine." He had a choice between the sea off Alexandria or the excavations of Cleopatra's Palace. He chose the latter and was thrown clear as the plane crumpled on a hillside. He walked back to the aerodrome and got into another aircraft with an instructor. So much for the timid Tasmanian boy of the pre-war years.

When war ended, he had survived Gallipoli, several land battles, two crashes, the German air force and a severe bout of influenza, during an epidemic that would soon kill millions around the world. He and McGinness had both won the Distinguished Flying Cross for gallantry in air combat. Fysh got his wings on 28 February 1919 and sailed for Australia five days later on the *Port Sydney*. Paul McGinness, who had survived no less harrowing scrapes, was also on board, as was Arthur Baird. Each pondered his future.

They were returning to a country that didn't quite know what to do with them, after the welcome home parades had gone by. Jobs were scarce and nerves frayed. From a population of five million, 300,000 men had enlisted; over 60,000 were killed and 156,000 were wounded, gassed or taken prisoner,

August 1919: George Gorham, Paul McGinness and Hudson Fysh, ready to set off from Longreach on their epic overland journey to Darwin.

most of these on the western front. Australian casualties in the Middle East were relatively light—1394 killed or wounded.

In No.1 Squadron, according to Fysh, 19 men were killed, two died, 23 were wounded and 12 taken prisoner, from a total roll call of 168 pilots and observers. In 1918, the squadron lost 12 planes through enemy action, eight through other causes; the enemy lost 29 planes and 53 were driven down.

In mid-April, the *Port Sydney* docked at Hobart and Fysh went home to his family at Launceston. He was 24, restless and unprepared for a post-war life. He had lost interest in wool classing. "Whatever would I do?" he asked himself.

McGinness had an idea. On March 19, 1919, while they were still at sea, the Australian government of William Morris Hughes announced it would award £10,000 to the first Australian who succeeded in flying from England to Australia within 720 consecutive hours before midnight on December 31, 1920. The aim was to "stimulate aerial activity". The dream of an eventual air route to London was already brewing. Among the conditions was that only one aircraft could be used and the finishing point would be the vicinity of Port Darwin.

McGinness and Fysh were keen, as was Arthur Baird. The problem was to find a backer. In Palestine, McGinness and Fysh had flown a Bristol Fighter donated by a wealthy NSW grazier, Sir Samuel McCaughey. McGinness went to Yanco to see him and got his agreement to finance their bid. Fysh sold the car he had bought and left for Melbourne. Baird agreed to join them. They made bookings to sail to England. Here was a great adventure to be tackled.

Other teams were forming, too. Bert Hinkler and Charles Kingsford Smith made separate plans, but neither would get a start. Most of those who did enter were veterans of the AFC, or Australians who had flown with the British. Some had survived the war only to die in this contest. Some would survive the contest only to die soon in other flying ventures. Six teams entered, but McGinness, Fysh and Baird weren't among them. Sir Samuel McCaughey died before they got the money. Their adventurous plans collapsed, but the idea for Qantas would eventually flow from this piece of bad luck.

Whoever won the contest would have to fly on past Darwin, so an aerial route had to be found, with suitable sites for refuelling, forced landings and detailed maps for navigating by sight. The Defence department asked McGinness and Fysh to survey the route between Longreach in western Queensland and Darwin. Baird went back to Melbourne, but the two younger men accepted, arriving in Longreach on August 14, 1919.

They set out four days later in a Model T Ford utility, with a local handyman, George Gorham, probably the only one who had some idea of what they were in for.

McGinness was leader; Fysh was to do the maps, notes and photographs. The journey was largely cross-country and they were warned that no car had ever

Graziers warned them of danger from hostile Aborigines, but they were more often their rescuers. Horse-power also developed a new meaning.

got through the terrain. Six months earlier, Reginald Lloyd and J.C. Marduel got through from Sydney to Darwin via Longreach, but they went the more accessible western route, through Camooweal, Brunette Downs and Newcastle Waters, and they used motorbikes and sidecars. Theirs was the first attempt to survey an aerial route across Australia, but questions remained about a more northerly route via Burketown. This was the job given to McGinness and Fysh.

One reason both men realised that an aerial service might work here was that they discovered first-hand how hard it was to cross in a motor car. The region was prosperous with cattle, but the railheads in Charleville, Longreach, Winton and Cloncurry were unconnected and what passed for roads became bogs in the wet. They could see that the flat country suited flying, especially if you needed to make a forced landing.

They made Burketown on the Gulf of Carpentaria in one week; the next 355 miles to Borroloola in the Northern Territory took 24 days, averaging 16 miles per day. They crossed six tidal rivers and over 40 creeks, great stretches of sand and thickly wooded bush. They ran short of food, water and patience. Hudson Fysh wrote that they were barely speaking to each other by the end of this stretch. They had been warned that there were hostile blacks on the route, but it was often local Aborigines who got them through, pushing the Model T. On one 20-mile sandy stretch, they hitched the car to two horses.

The next 515 miles to Katherine River was easier and they arrived on October 8, after 51 days and 1354 miles (2179 kms). They had come through yet another physical ordeal together and seen possibilities in the terrain. They continued to Darwin by train, where Fysh was instructed to stay on and prepare landing grounds at Darwin and Katherine for the racers.

McGinness and Gorham were sent back to Cloncurry, establishing landing grounds across the Barkly tablelands as they went. This was to be another epic journey.

The first racers left England on October 21 in a single-engine Sopwith Wallaby. Captain G.C. Matthews and Sergeant T.D. Kay took six months to get as far as Bali, where they crashed in a banana plantation. They were imprisoned in Yugoslavia for a time, accused of being Bolshevik spies. (Matthews later became a Qantas pilot). The other crews left in November, some with tragic results. Flying an Alliance PZ Endeavour, Captain Roger Douglas and Lieutenant J.S.L. Ross crashed a few minutes after take off; both were killed. Captain Hubert Wilkins, who would become a noted arctic explorer, left with Valdemar Rendle, Reginald Williams and Garnsey Potts, all lieutenants, in a Blackburn Kangaroo on November 21, 1919. They had to abandon their attempt in Crete after a forced landing. Captain Cedric Howell, an RFC ace and Lieut. C.H. Fraser, in a Martinsyde Type A Mark 1 crashed and drowned off Corfu on December 9. Lieut. Ray Parer and Lieut. John McIntosh took off on January 2, 1920, after the prize had been won. They eventually made it to Darwin on August 2, 1920 in a DH9a, to become the first to fly England to Australia in a single-engine machine.

The day after Howell and Fraser were killed, brothers Ross and Keith Smith, with Jim Bennett and Walter Shiers as mechanics, landed at the Fanny Bay landing ground which Hudson Fysh had prepared for them at Darwin. They had left Hounslow on November 12 in a Vickers Vimy, powered by two Rolls Royce Eagle VIII engines, covering 17,780 kms (11,060 miles) in 135 hours, 55 minutes. Fysh was the first to greet his old comrade, Ross Smith, handing him a bundle of 50 or more telegrams. Smith told him he didn't recognise him at first. "Where's your uniform?" he asked.

Fysh described the arrival as one of the most moving sights he ever saw. "No-one had ever flown across the world before".

Heroes welcomed: Ross Smith greets his old comrade-in-arms, Hudson Fysh, in Darwin, December 10, 1919.

Registered at the General Post Office, Melbourne, for transmission by post as a newspaper.

Aircraft

Editor and Sole Proprietor
Edward J. Hart

OFFICIAL JOURNAL OF ASSOCIATED AUSTRALIAN AERO CLUBS
OFFICIAL JOURNAL OF THE AUSTRALIAN FLYING CORPS ASSOCIATION
OFFICIAL JOURNAL OF THE INSTITUTION OF AERONAUTICAL ENGINEERS
OFFICIAL JOURNAL OF THE AUSTRALIAN AIRCRAFT TRADERS' ASSOCIATION
OFFICIAL JOURNAL OF THE BRITISH SCIENCE GUILD (Aerial Development Section)

Vol. 8, No. 5.   JANUARY 31, 1930.   Price, 1/-

AUSTRALIAN-BUILT, TWENTY YEARS AGO

20-h.p. biplane designed, built and flown in 1910 by Mr. John Robertson Duigan, of Terang, Vic. The machine, now housed in the Technical Museum, Melbourne, had a speed of 40 m.p.h. Details of construction and performance are given in this issue. The biplane, with Mr. Duigan at the stick, is here depicted during a successful demonstration at Bendigo Racecourse on May 3, 1911.

Aircraft magazine's 1930 commemoration of John Duigan's historic first flight, from a copy kept by George.

44

CHAPTER THREE

Gods and Gravity

t the start of the 21st century, it is hard to understand just how extraordinary the idea of flying was to someone living at the start of the 20th century.

From 1903, when Wilbur and Orville Wright made that first controlled powered flight at Kitty Hawk, North Carolina, aviation gripped the world's imagination. Flying was something that only birds, angels and gods could do. People like Lawrence Hargrave, the Australian whose experiments with box kites contributed so much to the design of the first aircraft, sought to defy both gods and gravity.

The earliest aviators discovered you could fly in a heavier-than-air machine; you just had to be prepared to risk your life. In that sense, aviation was partly a blood sport. Huge crowds attended aerial derbies in Europe in 1909 to see men fly. Some just came to see men die, and they did. Three pilots were killed in Europe in 1909; the next year, with many more derbies taking place, 26 died. At Vincennes near Paris on June 18, 1911, three pilots died in one day at the start of the 1000-mile Circuit of Europe race. The crowd was estimated at half a million.

Barely two years earlier, England and France had been enthralled when Frenchman Louis Bleriot pointed his tiny monoplane and his impressive moustache towards England and flew 38 kms across the English Channel. He finished at Dover with a crash landing, but still claimed the £1000 prize offered by the press baron Lord Northcliffe.

M. Bleriot's inelegant landing at Dover, after crossing the English Channel in 1909.

In Australia, on July 16, 1910, near Kyneton, Victoria, John R. Duigan made the first flight in an Australian-designed and built aircraft, a biplane powered by a 20-hp engine. He reached only 24 feet (7.32 m) but there were many others who flew further and faster in imported machines. The bug bit Australia hard, despite—or perhaps because of—the country's isolation.

In June 1919, the two British war flyers Captain John Alcock and Lieut. Arthur Whitten-Brown made the first non-stop air crossing of the Atlantic, from Newfoundland to Ireland, a distance of about 3100 kms (1930 miles) in a Vickers Vimy. They ended up nose down in an Irish peat bog, but £10,000 richer, courtesy of Northcliffe's *Daily Mail*, sponsors of the competition. (Alcock didn't get much time to enjoy it—he died in a crash at Rouen six months later).

The idea for the much more ambitious England to Australia race may have been given to Australian Prime Minister Billy Hughes in Paris, in February of 1919, while he was at the peace talks. In *Farther and Faster, Aviation's Adventuring Years, 1909–1939*, Terry Gwynn-Jones says some Australian Flying Corps men asked him to let them fly their machines home to Australia, rather than leave them to be scrapped. The Atlantic race was then in preparation. Hughes probably saw that a race could promote Australia to the world and stimulate aviation at home. He also made sure the prize money was no less than that offered by Lord Northcliffe.

Ross and Keith Smith, with Bennett and Shiers, used the Vickers Vimy because of Alcock and Brown's success. Like them, the two brothers were later knighted for their achievement—the two engineers were not, though they had been extraordinarily innovative in keeping the Vimy flying.

To Australians, it was more than a feat of endurance and engineering. Since white settlement, Australians had defined themselves by how far they lived from Europe and America. "The isolation and backwardness which had condemned previous generations of Australians to material and cultural inferiority were about to end," wrote Manning Clark in the epilogue to his final volume of *A History of Australia*. Even those who felt neither culturally nor materially inferior could see that this was a big thing.

At home in Ipswich, George Roberts and his brothers and sister followed the story with intense interest. They listened on their crystal radio sets and followed the press reports in the *Brisbane Courier* and the *Queensland Times*. They were even more excited when the Vimy, en route south from Darwin, had to stop in Charleville with engine and propeller trouble. Ipswich was a major industrial centre for Queensland, so the engine and propeller were sent there for repair.

George: "The Ipswich railway workshops could build anything, anything at all. The engine was removed and sent on a train to the Ipswich Railway workshops, and there they made a new propeller for it in the pattern shop; they made new connecting rods for the engine, which was a 12-cylinder Rolls Royce Eagle VIII. With our father, Norm and I went to see this engine being tested. I saw Ross Smith. I met Bennett there too. I have a photograph, which my father took, at the workshops. Ross Smith signed our photograph."

To a 10-year-old boy, this was like meeting your greatest idol. Ross Smith had been the most decorated Australian flyer in Palestine; he had flown T. E. Lawrence (Lawrence of Arabia) on clandestine missions. Now he had conquered half the world and arrived in Ipswich.

Other flyers dropped in too, sometimes literally. Some time in 1919, ex-war pilot Jack Treacy, whom George thinks may have been flying a BE2e, landed somewhat bumpily in Cribb's paddock. This may have been the first plane to land there.

George: "He came in from the north, across the Blackstone Road. His wing tip took off an ornamental piece of filigree on the corner guttering of a house and his wheels touched the road, which was above the paddock and he went under the telephone wires, over the fence and landed. Dad and Norm and I ran over to the aeroplane when he came to a stop and he started to try and get out, but he was full as a boot. Dad tried to help him out and he slipped through his hands. That wasn't unusual for Jack, not unusual at all, but I never heard of him crashing anywhere. Whether he saw those telephone wires or whether he only saw the fence and was just lucky, I don't know."

The Vimy's damaged propeller (bottom) and its replacement, made from Queensland maple.

After the war, many ex-flying corps pilots bought surplus machines cheaply and went barnstorming. Charles Kingsford Smith would fly into weekend shows to give joyrides at £1 a go, less if the girl was pretty. Crashes were frequent, but there

Jim Bennett (top left) tests the Vimy engine at the Ipswich railway workshops. Ross Smith signed Bert Roberts' photograph, which is dated February 3, 1920.

49

was no shortage of takers. There were also aerial derbies, where pilots would race the clock around airfield pylons for prize money.

"Any aerial derby that was on, if we could afford to go, we were into it," says George, but he and his brother never went joyriding. Their interest by now was in the flying machines, more than the flying. They had always loved anything with an engine. Now they wanted to look under the engine cowlings of every aircraft they saw.

From about 1923, when George was 14, they bought and reconditioned a succession of motorbikes: a British AJS, a classic American Indian 4, and an Australian Waratah (built at Leichhardt, Sydney) among them. They would ride their motorbikes the 52 kms (33 miles) to Eagle Farm aerodrome to see the aerial pageants and to witness the arrivals of various pioneering aviators, who were setting new records almost weekly.

The aerodrome was flood prone, so planes would sometimes land at nearby Eagle Farm racecourse. They were there when Squadron Leader Bert Hinkler arrived in March 1928, after becoming the first to fly solo from England to Australia. They were there again in June when Charles Kingsford Smith landed in the *Southern Cross*, with co-pilot Charles Ulm, radio operator James Warner and navigator Harry Lyon, both Americans. These were the first to cross the Pacific in any direction by air. Their flight created headlines around the world, not least because many experts thought it was suicidal.

"For Smithy, Norm and I were there at Eagle Farm aerodrome by 3 a.m. No one knew what time they were going to be in. There was practically nobody else there at the time and we were lined up against the fence till 10 a.m., when the aircraft finally arrived. By this time we couldn't have gotten away from the fence if we wanted to because they had piled up so much behind us. We were following it on the radio and in the newspapers. We were doting on it. This was tremendous news."

Conquerors of the oceans: Charles Kingsford Smith and Charles Ulm arrive at Eagle Farm aerodrome in the Southern Cross, June 1928.

Bert Hinkler, the quiet achiever, whom George would meet later in Bundaberg.

Smith and Ulm share the kudos with their American navigator Harry Lyon and radio operator Jim Warner (right), during a tumultuous parade through Brisbane's streets.

Smithy and co had flown 11,600 kms (7,200 miles) in 83 hours in a Fokker F VIII trimotor, previously called *Detroiter*. It was the same plane Hubert (later Sir Hubert) Wilkins had used for Arctic exploration two years earlier, but they had converted it into a "flying fuel tank" capable of carrying 1300 gallons of fuel. The engines were so loud they could not talk to each other in-flight, nor hear much of what anyone said to them on arriving. The cheers of 15,000 people at Brisbane fell on temporarily deaf ears.

Two years later, Amy Johnson became the first woman to fly solo from Britain to Australia. The by-now well established Qantas sent a plane to escort her from Darwin to Brisbane, a DH50J piloted by C.W.A. Scott, but her arrival at Eagle Farm on May 29, 1930 was nearly a disaster.

Amy Johnson, looking happier than she did when George and Ivor Morris pulled her from her upturned Gipsy Moth on arrival in Brisbane.

Captain C.W.A. Scott, the Qantas pilot who guided Johnson to Eagle Farm. In 1935, he and T. Campbell Black flew from England to Melbourne in 70 hours, 54 minutes in a de Havilland Comet to win the Centenary Air Race.

George: "Charlie got impatient with her for dropping down to look at things along the way, like bunches of emus and kangaroos, so when he arrived at Eagle Farm aerodrome, he put his wheels down and gunned it straight off again, as if to say 'well there it is, you land there'. She duly put her wheels down in the same spot but it was too near the boundary fence. She tried to pull up but her wheels hit the top rail of a three-rail fence and the plane flipped over on its back and landed in a corn field.

"Norm and I had come down with our great pals, the Morris boys, who lived opposite us. Ivor Morris and I were the only ones watching from that end of the field. We were nearest to her when she crashed, so we raced to the aircraft (a Gipsy Moth called *Jason*), only a few feet away really, and she was hanging upside down there, harnessed into the cockpit.

"We helped her down out of the harness and sat her up on the ground. She was not unconscious but she wasn't sure where she was either. She didn't say anything and other people quickly came and picked her up and put her in the back seat of a car and drove her around the aerodrome to show she was alright.

"The other thing I can remember is that the man who owned the corn field was most irate at the number of people who had come in and trampled his corn down."

At the age of 15, George followed his elder brother into the family business, apprenticing first in his grandfather's coachbuilding business, then his father's motor dealership, which also did repairs. His first job was as a blacksmith's striker, belting white-hot pieces of metal with a sledgehammer, day in, day out.

"The blacksmith's name was Clarrie O'Brien and one of the first things he said to me when I took up the sledgehammer was 'when I nod my head, you hit it'. But I never did."

A year earlier, with what was becoming a seven-year curse, George had almost died again.

"I was at the seaside and I got sick again and it was put down to some fish I had eaten. We left the seaside and returned through Brisbane on our way to Ipswich and I became ill. They took me to a friend's home and there, I lapsed into a coma. I was taken to hospital and it was diagnosed as ptomaine poisoning. Some put it down to fish that had been left in the moonlight—that was a story at the time. I was very sick for a while, but I came through it satisfactorily."

Any parent would have found this distressing. Flo Roberts must have found it chilling. Two years earlier, she had lost her five-month-old baby boy, Trevor.

George: "He died in my arms as I was walking the hall, trying to keep him going. The story was that he initially got enteritis and that finished up as meningitis. At least that was the diagnosis at the time, whether it was correct or otherwise I would not know. He was born in 1921, so I would have been 12, I suppose. I knew he had died. I have often wondered how I felt about it at the time. I don't know. But I can still recall that day, being in the hallway, walking with Trevor in my arms.

"My mother never overcame that. That was one thing that was very obvious, that my mother never overcame that. My father had a nice gold brooch made for her with the word Trevor on it and I saw that on her, pinned to her, for the rest of her life. It was always there."

Despite these traumas, Flo Roberts still did not try to curtail her children's sometimes dangerous adventures.

George: "After that experience with the glider, where it crashed, although there were no injuries, we felt that we should learn how to fall. There were 13 front stairs on our home, directly in front of the hallway, and in our teens we would run down this hallway, jump the length of the stairs and roll over at the bottom, learning to somersault. This we felt was part of what we should do if we were going to learn to fly an aeroplane. It was quite a jump. My mother didn't stop us doing that; she felt that that was something we ought to do. She was a very affectionate mother indeed, very much so."

A year or two later, George was out in the world, earning a living. He had enjoyed school, but when he was offered the choice at 15 to go on to grammar school or start his apprenticeship, he chose the latter.

The blacksmithing helped him to recover from the effects of the ptomaine poisoning, and he grew physically strong. He needed to be fit, working under a galvanised iron roof with the heat of the forges during an Ipswich summer.

George: "It was very very hot indeed. We wore black clothes and at the forge we always wore a leather apron. I learned one thing very early in the piece—when you're first striking the anvil with a very heavy sledgehammer, you don't know how to handle it and you grip the handle too tightly. The result is the fingers then lock on to the handle and won't move. You can't open your hand. So there was a water barrel alongside where everything was quenched, and you took the hammer with both hands into the water and opened your hands underwater and that did it. You learned then not to hold the handle too tightly."

He also learned skills which are now virtually forgotten: how to weld in the forge, how to shrink metal tyres onto the wheels of the sulkies, buggies, drays and phaetons his grandfather was building, precision woodwork for the carriage bodies, how to do fancy painting and varnishing. He and Norm also took classes at the Ipswich Technical College, learning automotive engineering. George did fitting and machining by day, bookkeeping, shorthand and typing by night. He was fascinated by auto instruments, so he did extra classes in electrics, learning about magnetos, speedometers, generators, distributors, starter motors and oil pressure gauges. His later work with aircraft instruments at Qantas would grow directly out of this study.

"My father supplied the ambulance in Ipswich with Oakland vehicles and my grandfather built the ambulance bodies for them. Very often that body was changed to a new chassis, because of the distances they were doing, and my father gave several of these chassis to the technical college, so it became a class to restore them fully, the engine, differential, gearbox, the whole lot."

By their late teens, they could strip, repair, rebuild and soup up almost any car they were given. Over the next five years, they built twelve cars from scratch, modifying the engines to make them go faster and giving them sports car bodies. They were hotrodders before that term was in use.

"These cars were based on the Model T Ford and we bought new Rajo and Frontignac Ford replacement parts in Brisbane. These were special cylinder heads, larger, more robust crankshafts, lighter pistons and connecting rods. We made patterns and had castings made to produce lowering brackets, so we could lower the cars considerably. You had to lower the centre of gravity to obtain higher speeds. When Ford discontinued the Model T in 1927, parts from those were very cheap. We were buying a very robust wire wheel in sets of five, plus hubs and brake drums, for £4 per set, as replacements for the original wooden wheels. We built these before and during the Depression years (from 1929) and sold them to friends who had more monies than ourselves; they were a means of getting some funds together."

They were also a way of having even more dangerous fun.

"The standard Model T Ford normally operated at around 35 mph, but we took one of our Rajos down onto Main Beach at Southport, before

Boy racers: George, their cousin Bill Pearce and Don Roberts in an underslung Fronti Ford in 1932. George and Norm built the car themselves.

Surfer's Paradise ever existed, and drove it along the beach at 104 mph. I was driving and I was quite pleased with it, but as for braking, there was very little braking associated with that vehicle. We certainly had brakes, but not adequate for those speeds."

George remembers the local policeman being reluctant to get in one of these vehicles when he eventually went to get his driver's licence, at age 17. He had been driving for ten years by this stage.

"It was a rainy day, not particularly heavy, but I went up to the police station and the sergeant who was going to take me for my driving licence looked at the vehicle and he said: 'you get in the vehicle, you drive up to the next corner, you do a U-turn there, come back past me to the next corner, do another U-turn and return to me', which I did. He wasn't going to get into an open-wheeled vehicle and be covered in mud from the dirt roads of those days."

In that first year out of school, George and Norm began building their first real aircraft, after the disastrous glider.

"The first plane was entirely built of timber, all spruce, Canadian spruce. That timber was available from the same source that my grandfather used for timber to build vehicles, bus bodies and utilities. Likewise the plywood that we used, which was known as aircraft ply, that also came from Canada. The design came from drawings in *Popular Mechanics*. It didn't fly, because we didn't have an engine for it, but it remained in the old home in the garage, strung up in the rafters for many years until it became so rotten that I finally destroyed it."

George emerged from his apprenticeship just as the Depression hit Australia hard.

"When I came out we were running into the Depression years and my father, attempting to keep the business operating, mortgaged the home, but finally the business closed and so also did the coachworks. As a result of the Depression, people stopped buying cars and those people that had motorcars also stopped repairing them. Homes were just out of money, completely out of money. It became an era where people would walk miles and miles to get a job. When this happened, it was obvious to both Norm and I and to our father that we had to do something else to keep the family going, because we had a younger sister and a younger brother. My father had the idea of a service station and he obtained a block of land from the council on the corner of a park known as the Five Ways. There, my brother Norm and I physically built the station."

This meant digging the three large holes required for the tanks—each about 3.6 metres square and deep (12 feet). They dug these through basalt with a pick and shovel.

"I would say at that time we were very strong, both Norm and I. Norm didn't do the blacksmithing that I did, but we were both exceptionally strong, I would think, for our ages, because of the type of work we did.

Do-It-Yourself. George and Norm built the service station as well as the car. Norm is driving the Fronti Ford, their friend Eric Freer is the passenger and George is standing. 1932.

The first Roberts plane (after the glider) takes shape in the backyard at 7 York Street. It never flew because they couldn't afford an engine. Norm on left, George on right.

It was not unusual for either of us to lift a car. The wheels were unlike the cars today, they were all spoke wheels, larger wheels, but if we wanted to put a jack or a block under the axle, one would go lift the wheel, the other would put the block under the axle and that was it. It was not unusual, but we always did it with our back to the wheel."

The service station didn't pay them wages but it made enough to keep food on the table and the two youngest children at school. To earn pocket money, the brothers did other work after hours: George repaired gramophones and made metal reeds for musical instruments for Palings, the music emporium. Both boys took a course in non-ferrous metal welding in Brisbane, a skill that was then rare. They needed this when John Morris, father of their best friends Humphrey and Ivor Morris, asked them to modify the machinery at his woollen mill at Redbank. The antiquated machinery was from a defunct Scottish mill. George and Norm converted it all from belt-driven to mechanical operation, using differentials from cheap second-hand Ford one-ton trucks. (When he visited this same mill in 1995, George noted that the scouring machines were still running off these same 70-year-old differentials).

Still, the Depression got worse. This extra money was not enough to cover the mortgage their father took out. Now, Bert Roberts faced losing the family home.

George: "Towards the end of the war, my dad had been very helpful to a man we knew as Old Dad Little. He had come to my dad and said he had no money, but he could see the opportunity for a bus run in Ipswich if he could be provided with vehicles. Prior to that, there were no motor buses, only horse-drawn coaches. My dad agreed that he would provide the first vehicle on a promissory note and that Mr Little would at least give him the deposit of that within three months. So my father produced the chassis and my grandfather built the body on that first bus. Old Dad Little drove the bus and people flocked to it. The result was that not only did he come back in three months and pay what he owed, but he ordered three more buses. The bus run just took off, and of course, it killed off the horse-drawn coaches."

Twelve years later, Old Dad Little's son-in-law, David Boyce, came to see Bert Roberts.

"He said to my father, 'I believe you're in trouble with your home, Mr Roberts?' Dad said 'yes, I am. I took out a loan on it to try to keep the business going and I can't repay that.' David said 'how much is it?' Dad told him and David said 'well, here's the money'. He said 'I wouldn't be in a job today running buses, which have continued to make money through the Depression, if you hadn't assisted my father-in-law previously'. David Boyce loaned him the money to pay out the debt on the house and that saved the house."

Depression decency: Bert Roberts helped "Dad" Little establish Ipswich's first motor bus service. Twelve years later, that generosity saved the Roberts family home.

Outback turkey shoot: McGinness (left) and Fysh with a wild turkey shot from the air at the appropriately named Wellshot station. The plane is the BE2e.

CHAPTER FOUR

Friends in High Places

In July 1920, Bert Roberts had a visit from a man representing the Perdriau Rubber Company. They made tyres at Birkenhead Point in Sydney.

George: "Jack Butler flew up in a BE2e and asked my dad to take up the dealership for Perdriau tyres, which he did. He landed in Brisbane and also in Cribb's paddock in Ipswich. He wanted to advertise the tyres by dropping pamphlets over Brisbane and Ipswich and Norm and I were elected to do that. He flew the plane, with us two kids in the other cockpit, which was open, and we threw these pamphlets out over Brisbane and Ipswich. Today they would call it pollution, wouldn't they? That became our second flight. I still have one of those pamphlets today and that BE2e became Qantas's second aircraft."

Fergus McMaster.

This was still before there was a Qantas, but the idea was brewing. In the early months of 1920, after an arduous return journey from Darwin, Paul McGinness set about talking up his plans for an aerial service with local graziers. Many were enthusiastic but it was a chance meeting with Fergus McMaster, then managing Devoncourt station near Cloncurry for his sick brother, which proved decisive.

McMaster broke a front axle of his car one Sunday afternoon crossing the Cloncurry River. McGinness was about to head off to a picnic with a young woman when McMaster came up the street towards him. The two men had met briefly before. If McGinness had gone to that picnic, instead of offering to help McMaster fix his car, there might never have been a Qantas. What the young woman thought about having to go to the picnic with someone else is not known.

McMaster said later that McGinness's generosity and resourcefulness impressed him. Faced with a succession of locked garages, McGinness just removed a sheet of corrugated iron from a garage wall to get the parts he needed.

McMaster was in his mid-30s, recently returned from Europe after demobilisation. He had been a gunner in the AIF on the western front, among the worst positions you could get into in that war. He had fought at Amiens, Villers-Bretonneux and Hamel.

In England, before sailing for home, he had taken a 10-minute joyride flight at Hendon, so he was probably one of few men in western Queensland who had actually flown. When McGinness and Fysh came to see him in Brisbane

The historic and elegant Gresham Hotel in Brisbane, since demolished.
It stood at the corner of Adelaide and Creek streets.

in June 1920, the fact that he had flown may have made him more receptive than other ground-loving graziers. This was soon after Fysh arrived back in Cloncurry, after a difficult return journey from Darwin.

McMaster was staying at the elegant Gresham Hotel. He listened to their proposition for an aerial taxi service, to be supplemented with income from joyriding. McGinness had probably become an expert at pitching—he had already spent six months spruiking to other outback men of means.

McMaster liked their ideas and their enthusiasm, and being war veterans helped considerably. In fact he probably saw more in the venture than they did. Air routes between Sydney, Melbourne and Adelaide had been surveyed throughout 1919, and faster mail services were a primary goal of the new industry of aviation. The 20th century was already speed-obsessed.

The first prospectus for the new company, printed in October 1920, outlined ambitious plans for an aerial mail service from Longreach to Port Darwin, via Winton, Cloncurry, Avon Downs, Anthony Lagoon, Newcastle Waters and Katherine. In *The Defeat of Distance*, the first volume of John Gunn's meticulous history of Qantas, he says this would have been "the longest direct air service in the world". The prospectus also predicted that the government would assist the venture, especially as it had implications for the defence of Australia.

Thus, the idea had grown well beyond the taxi and joyriding concept. The name changes throughout 1920 show that they were struggling with these new ideas. The first name was Western Queensland Auto Aero Service Ltd, which would have yielded an ugly acronym like "Weqaas". The next name was the much grander Australian Transcontinental Aerial Services Company Ltd, which could have become "Atasco", except that the new company was neither Australia-wide nor transcontinental. When the company was formally registered in Brisbane on November 16, 1920, it was with a more modest and accurate name—Queensland and Northern Territory Aerial Services Ltd.

McMaster's backing was crucial, because he was well connected, both in politics and pasture. His way of helping was old school and practical: he asked his friends for money, starting with Ainslie Templeton, of Acacia Downs station near Longreach, who was also staying at the Gresham. McMaster wrote later that he did not present it as a sure thing. "There was no doubt in my mind that although the venture of an air service in the outback was not a gilt-edged investment, aviation should be encouraged."

Templeton offered to match whatever McMaster put in, but in fact doubled it, to £1000. McGinness put in the same, then another £200, making

The Australian Aircraft and Engineering Company at 12 Bridge Street, Mascot. Below: At right, the Qantas 504K takes shape; at left, the chassis of a Calthorpe Minor motor car.

him the largest shareholder. Fysh and McMaster put up £500 each, with Fysh soon adding another £100. The full capital by May 1921 was £6850. They would need every penny.

At a second meeting at the Gresham in August, the flyers were authorised to buy some aeroplanes. They ordered two Avro 504Ks from the

Australian Aircraft and Engineering Company in Mascot, Sydney, a new company started by Nigel Love, an ex-war pilot and H.E. Broadsmith, an engineer, in 1919. They were making planes under licence from A.V. Roe in England.

In Melbourne after the failure of the air race bid, Arthur Baird had started a garage in Lygon Street, Carlton. He now took a major gamble, sold the garage and met Fysh and McGinness in Sydney. Baird would also put £50 into the new venture.

The Avro could carry a pilot and two passengers, but the order called for the usual Clerget rotary engines to be replaced with Sunbeam Dyak engines. These were water-cooled and more reliable but they took over three months to come from England. The planes were to cost £1500 each, half the company's capital, but until they were ready, no money was coming in.

By the time the first Avro was delivered in late January 1921, they had cancelled the order for the second Avro Dyak in favour of the brand new Avro triplane, which was nearly twice the price, but could carry four passengers. While they were waiting, Charles Knight, a Longreach stock and station agent, asked McGinness and Fysh if they could fly his new plane home. He had bought one of the two BE2e planes imported by the Perdriau Rubber Company, but he couldn't fly it. This was the aircraft in which Jack Butler had taken George and Norm Roberts to bomb Brisbane with advertising.

The new company got airborne on January 31, 1921, when McGinness took off from Mascot in the new Avro Dyak, heading for Winton. Fysh left in the BE2e with Baird, which was an act of faith by both men, since Fysh had only 30 minutes flying time and one landing in that kind of aircraft.

The first leg was hair-raising. En route to Singleton, in deteriorating weather, Fysh took on some thick cloud, went into a spin and had to make a forced landing on a hillside near the Red Head coal mine. A miner's wife gave them a cup of tea while they waited for the clouds to clear. They overnighted in Moree, then St George, where they delayed a few days while Baird fixed a fault. At Barcaldine, McGinness picked up a nervous Fergus McMaster for the leg to Longreach. The next day, February 7, 1921, Templeton joined McMaster as a passenger in the Avro. They were both supposed to know the way to Winton, but things looked different from the air. They got lost. A flight which should have taken 90 minutes took three hours and they landed in front of a large crowd (for Winton) with barely 15 minutes of fuel left. The party celebrated with much needed refreshments at the original North Gregory Hotel. The rule about pilots not drinking, which was later to become a major disagreement within the company, had not yet been written.

Longreach stock and station agent Charles Knight (left) with Hudson Fysh and the BE2e. After a rough flight on February 7, 1921, Knight swore never to fly again and sold the plane to Qantas.

Fysh's passenger on that flight was Charles Knight, owner of the BE2e. On the return to Longreach, in very rough conditions, Fysh got lost, Knight got sick and Qantas got a new aeroplane, when Knight vowed never to fly again. The BE2e was theirs for £450.

Qantas now had everything it needed, except passengers and capital. The government rejected its first application for a subsidy and McGinness crashed the Avro triplane during tests in Sydney. This was the plane with which they had hoped to start a commercial service between Winton and Longreach. Fysh kept the company aloft with joyriding, at £3 and three shillings a 10-minute turn. McGinness soon joined him. In the first four months, Fysh lifted 296 passengers, clocking 98 hours in the air. McGinness carried 285 passengers, in 111 hours. Between them, they brought in £1771.

The company headquarters moved from Winton to Longreach, 160 kms to the south east, within a month of the planes arriving. Longreach was

Hudson Fysh washes outback grime from the BE2e at Thargomindah in 1921.
Note the well swept runway.

bigger and it had Herb Avery's Western Motor Works, where Baird could use the workshop for machining and repairs. The company had no hangar and no real aerodrome. The office was some free space in Frank Cory's stock and station agency, a wood and galvanised iron building on Duck Street. They landed almost in the town itself, beside the showground. Baird set up a shelter here, to keep the weather off the planes.

Joyriding was an exciting if improvisational business. Fysh would fly to a small town with Herb Avery as mechanic; Baird flew with McGinness. They would land on roads, paddocks or clay pans. At Thargomindah, Fysh arrived to find hundreds of residents sweeping a clay pan with brooms. Their telegram had requested a landing area free of stones and potholes.

They were sometimes paid in "shinplasters", IOUs redeemable at a local pub. At the Urandangi picnic races, McGinness conducted joyflights and rode the winner in one of the races. At the Cunnamulla races, Fysh was engaged to fly over local stations and drop boxes of chocolates addressed to local beauties. He carried small homemade parachutes to assist the chocolates' landing and the process of outback courting. At another station, he took the manager up to shoot wild turkeys. The owner of the station sacked the manager on their return.

At night the plane had to be pegged to the ground, lest the wind flip it over. Fysh would hire a nightwatchman, "usually some old deadbeat", to sleep under the wing, keeping off souvenir hunters and cows and horses, which liked to chew the wings.

The joyriding went well until August 2, 1921 when McGinness crashed the Avro Dyak into a canefield at Ingham, after his throttle lever broke. He was uninjured but the plane was badly damaged, eating up the profits they had made. The triplane was still under repair in Sydney, so the company now had precisely one plane, the BE2e, capable of carrying one passenger.

With their backs to the wall, the directors began a desperate rescue campaign of propaganda, politics and an increased overdraft. McGinness, Fysh and McMaster set out across the length and breadth of Queensland, by plane, train and automobile, to drum up new shareholders and civic support for a subsidised aerial mail service between Cloncurry and Charleville. They had new leaflets printed proclaiming "Flying's the Thing". They sent out a new prospectus aiming to raise £15,000 and hired a professional share-raiser, a man named Clarkson. Fysh chased one wealthy grazier, Mr T. A. Stirton, along a country road till he caught him and persuaded him to subscribe for 200 shares.

McGinness flew the Avro after a train when Mr C. Foy of Sydney, who owned a station in Longreach, left his satchel behind in the Longreach Club. McGinness signalled the driver until he stopped, then dropped the bag from the Avro. Mr Foy later bought 750 shares.

On August 2, the Commonwealth had approved a £25,000 subsidy for an aerial service between Geraldton and Derby in Western Australia (awarded to Norman Brearley's Western Australian Airways) and tenders had been called for Sydney-Brisbane and Sydney-Adelaide services. McMaster rallied his contacts in the Country Party to lobby the government for a similar thing for western Queensland. Telegrams arrived at the Prime Minister's office in Melbourne from many Queensland shire and town councils, chambers of commerce and community groups. On November 10, Billy Hughes finally met a delegation in his office, consisting of McMaster and all Queensland members from both Houses of Parliament. He gave them a flat "no", saying the government had no money for aerial subsidies. What he probably meant was "no money for you lot", because he was in the middle of a power struggle with the Country Party, which had been voting solidly with the Labour party for reductions in the government estimates.

McGinness now took bold and direct action. When "a certain member of the government" who might well have been Hughes, took the train from Melbourne to Sydney, McGinness got in to talk to him and made a deal. McGinness phoned McMaster from a railway station en route to say that if the Country Party would ease its opposition on the estimates, money for a subsidy could probably be found. The Country Party member for Maranoa, Mr A. J. Hunter, a close friend of McMaster's, told the House on November 22 that if unexpended funds were to be used to subsidise commercial aviation, "it would probably induce Honourable Members to pass these estimates as they stand".

Within a week of this about-face, McMaster was told that tenders would be called soon for a Charleville-Cloncurry service.

Qantas was by no means assured of winning. They needed more capital and more planes quickly. There was strong competition from the Larkin Aircraft Supply Company, which had won the Sydney-Brisbane and Sydney-Adelaide contracts. Worse, the Controller of Civil Aviation, Lieut. Colonel H.C. Brinsmead, wanted large aircraft to be used. He favoured the heavy and untried Vickers Vulcan, which could carry eight passengers. Qantas, which knew there could be problems with overheating engines in the western climate, wanted the smaller DH9C. In the end, Qantas tendered for two Vulcans and a smaller DH4, which they bought from Ray Parer in Melbourne for £1500.

Qantas won the tender, worth £12,000 a year, on February 2, 1922. The next nine months would prove tougher than anyone expected.

The Avro triplane, when finally repaired and tested, was judged unsafe. It had cost over £3000 and had to be junked. The engine was sent to Longreach but the fuselage ended up as a chicken coop in a suburban Sydney home, according to Fysh. The Vickers machines were delayed by strikes; when finally tested in England, they did not meet the required performance standards. Brinsmead had stipulated that Qantas must recruit a third pilot in England with experience on heavier machines; Vickers could not find anyone prepared to go, especially as McMaster had insisted they must sign the pledge not to drink. When the DH4 arrived in Longreach, Baird discovered it needed a complete overhaul. With the Vickers planes delayed, Qantas bought two Armstrong Whitworth FK-8 machines from Melbourne, but these also needed modifications. The company was living on credit as hangars were built and aerodromes prepared. In 1922, Qantas lost £4,400.

The start-up for the Charleville-Cloncurry service was delayed until September 26, then October 5, then November 2. A week before this date, Paul McGinness floored everyone by cabling his resignation. Several factors have been cited, but there is no direct record from McGinness.

In *Qantas Rising*, published in 1964, Fysh notes that the board on July 8, 1922 gave Fysh charge of flying operations and control of the company's aerodromes and hangars. Baird was designated 'aerodrome manager'. Marcus Griffin, an accountant with a distinguished war record, had been recruited as manager during May. Did McGinness feel passed over by these appointments? He had been the one who was so crucial in the negotiations in Melbourne, he and Clarkson had raised much of the new capital the company was living on; indeed, the whole idea for the company was his. What was his role now to be—chief pilot?

Fysh does not say that McGinness was disappointed. He wrote only that McGinness "seemed to be getting on the outer, for he could not add any showing of administrative ability to his many great qualities".

It is known that he disagreed with the anti-drinking rule. McGinness

Longreach welcome; McGinness and Baird arriving after the first scheduled
Qantas airmail flight from Charleville. McGinness's decision to quit remains a puzzle.

had tried to get the board to agree that pilots be allowed to drink nothing stronger than beer, but he was the only one who voted for it. Clarkson's services had been terminated earlier in the year once enough shares had been subscribed; McGinness would later take up with him on a share-raising job in Western Australia, the first of many unsuccessful business and farming ventures McGinness would go through post-Qantas. Meanwhile, he agreed to stay on to pilot the first commercial Qantas flight.

That took place as scheduled at 5.30 a.m. on November 2, 1922, almost two years after the company had been registered.

A good crowd of Charleville residents gathered to hear the mayor farewell McGinness and Baird in the Armstrong Whitworth FK-8, registered as G-AUDE. McGinness told them this service was destined to link Australia to Asia, Europe, Africa and Great Britain. He was more right than he could have known. Longreach was only 428 kms away (266 miles), but this was the start of something big. His foresight makes his departure all the more poignant and puzzling.

Alexander Kennedy was the first passenger on a scheduled Qantas flight, travelling from Longreach to Cloncurry. He is shown here on a later trip in the DH61, which had an enclosed cabin.

McGinness piloted the FK-8 from Longreach to Charleville on its return after the inaugural flight, with Miss Ivy McLain as the second paying passenger. Jack Hazlett, with mail bag, was the engineer. McGinness left the company soon after.

Their cargo on the first leg was 106 letters and no passengers. They stopped at Tambo and Blackall en route and arrived in Longreach ahead of schedule at 10.15 a.m., to a cheering crowd. Whether McGinness took a drink that night is not recorded.

Fysh piloted the second leg the next day, with 84-year-old Alexander Kennedy on board. A pioneer of the district, he had been one of the first to listen to McGinness's plan two years earlier and he had subscribed 250 shares on the promise that he could be the first paying passenger.

Unfortunately, the second FK-8, which was experiencing a loss of power in its engine, refused to take off. Fysh tried three times then transferred to G-AUDE. As they finally left the black soil of Longreach bound for Cloncurry, via Winton and McKinlay, Kennedy is said to have shouted from the open cockpit, his white beard flapping in the wind: "Be damned to the doubters".

In 1926, the then 88-year-old Alexander Kennedy was still flying regularly on Qantas services. He is seen here in a DH9C, in a cockpit which Arthur Baird modified with a canopy. Baird is in the cockpit at right loading baggage.

Bush repairs: Mechanic Frank McNally gets a lift from Qantas manager Marcus Griffin at Tambo, Queensland in 1923. The aircraft is an Armstrong Whitworth FK-8.

CHAPTER FIVE

Growing Pains

George and Norm decided as teenagers that their future was in aviation. Being Queenslanders, they set their sights on working for the Queensland airline.

George: "We knew all about Qantas from its earliest days. We read about it in the newspapers. There was a pictorial magazine called *The Queenslander* and we learned a lot about it from that. Both Norm and I had the thought that since our grandfather started in horse-drawn carriages and our father migrated into the motor business, it was really up to us then to migrate into aircraft. That was the natural progression that we should follow in transport."

At 18, Norm tried to enlist in the Royal Australian Air Force, but his father put his foot down. "When Norm gave him the papers to sign, Dad refused. He said 'I'm not signing your death warrant'."

Qantas was having troubles that the boys were unlikely to see reported in *The Queenslander*.

The first two years after scheduled services began were touch-and-go, with constant engine problems and a shortage of suitable aircraft. There were 17 forced landings in the first year of the mail contract. Increasing pilot experience and modifications to the aircraft reduced this to three in the next eight months. The arrival of two used DH9C aircraft in late 1923 helped to stabilise the company.

By 1928, Qantas was modestly profitable, with a good, if not unblemished, safety record. (In March 1927, pilot A.D. Davidson and two passengers were killed when a DH9C stalled and crashed at Tambo, the airline's first fatal crash).

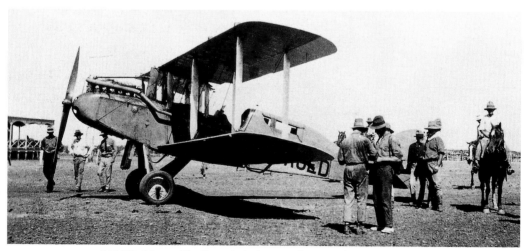

A DH9C at Townsville. The arrival of two used DH9Cs in late 1923 helped the airline's precarious situation.

Which way to the terminal?
Qantas's first passenger facilities at Roma.

Qantas operated flying schools in Brisbane from 1927 and Longreach from 1926, when it also began building aircraft under Arthur Baird's supervision. The first was the DH50, a four-passenger workhorse made under licence from de Havilland. In 1928 Qantas also began an historic collaboration with John Flynn to run an aerial outback medical service—what would become the Royal Flying Doctor Service.

Mail services had already been extended to Normanton on the Gulf of Carpentaria and Camooweal in the Northern Territory, but Qantas was still only an outback airline.

Isolation had been the mother of the idea, but it had many drawbacks, such as getting experienced people to live in Longreach. Fergus McMaster could see that it had to expand or die, but the Commonwealth did not want to subsidise air services on routes already covered by its own railways. It would take Qantas almost a decade to get access to a capital city route.

In 1929, Norman Brearley began an Adelaide-Perth service, which made Western Australian Airways the country's premier airline, according to the magazine, *Aircraft*. In January 1930, Kingsford Smith and Charles Ulm began a Brisbane-Sydney service without a subsidy, an unprecedented move. It proved an immediate, if short-lived success.

The break for Qantas came in 1928, when the Commonwealth finally decided to call tenders for a service between Charleville and Brisbane.

The Wool Exchange building, the first Qantas office in Brisbane.

Norm, George, Don and Ivy, circa 1932, at home. The trees have grown and so have they. George's new suit is made from cloth from the Ipswich Woollen Mills.

Once again, Fysh and McMaster put together a skilful bid. They beat the competition, even though their price was higher, because they had ordered larger aircraft: two DH61s, the 'Giant Moth', which could carry eight passengers —just what the Civil Aviation Board, still then a section of the Department of Defence, had wanted.

The service began in April 1929, again with Alexander Kennedy, now 91, as a passenger. The new Brisbane office opened in June in the Wool Exchange building in Eagle Street. Qantas already had a hangar at Eagle Farm aerodrome. Hudson Fysh and Arthur Baird moved to Brisbane. Lester Brain, who in 1924 had been the first non-war pilot to join the company, ran the Brisbane Flying School until May 1929, when it was handed to the Queensland Aero Club. He now became chief pilot. Qantas's bush flying days were far from over, but it now had its capital city toehold.

George Roberts was 20 when Qantas moved to Brisbane. On the eve of his 21st birthday, the seven year cycle of illness struck again, with more force.

He was overhauling an engine at home when a severe stomach pain hit.

"I found I couldn't continue to stand up so with the block and tackle I put the engine on the floor, laid down beside it and worked on the engine that way."

The pain subsided, only to return that night. "About 3 a.m., my brother Norm came to my bed and asked me what was wrong. I told him I was in terrible pain, so he woke the family and I was escorted to hospital. I had a burst appendix and by the time I got into hospital, they considered it had been 11 hours since the appendix had burst."

George remembers a doctor asking his father if his son drank spirits. "The doctor said the only thing I can now attempt with him is whisky. But whether that whisky was put down my throat or onto the wound during the operation I don't know because by this time I was unconscious."

He underwent three operations, as the doctors fought to drain and cleanse his system. He remembers fainting at one point from the stench made by the infection. "Finally after nine weeks in hospital, I came out of it and came home. My doctor, Dr Simmonds, who had dealt with my other problems

The Wicko Cabin Sports, stripped down for transport behind one of the home-made Fronti Fords. George took the photo in Ipswich, after the aeroplane had been test flown at Archerfield.

*George Roberts, pilot, 1932. George and Norm learned to fly at Archerfield
in the early 1930s. Seen here in his dashing military reserve uniform, George is about to take
a Gipsy Moth for a spin.*

Kindred spirits: Geoff Wikner, right, with Norm and the Wicko Wizard, the second of three aircraft the Roberts brothers helped to build. George took the photo.

said to me: 'Well, seven, 14, 21. What's going to happen to you at 28? Maybe you'll get married'."

Before the illness George and his brother discovered a kindred soul in Geoff Wikner, a man five years their senior who was desperate to design, build and fly his own aircraft. Wikner was an adventurous, restless spirit, struggling

The Wicko Wizard in Brisbane in 1934, in front of Qantas hangar No. 1. Wikner left for England soon after, where he designed and built a series of aircraft.

as a refrigeration mechanic by day, building gliders and aeroplanes at night and weekends. George and Norm helped him build the first of his designs on the third floor of a warehouse in Parbury Lane, off Eagle Street in Brisbane.

"There was no lift but there was a lift well so we lowered this aircraft down through the lift well on the rope, block and tackle to the ground floor. Then we put it on a trailer and towed it out to Archerfield and reassembled it."

This aircraft, which he called the Wicko Cabin Sports, first flew at the new Archerfield aerodrome on January 25, 1931, but George missed it. He was still in hospital.

It was a high-wing cabin monoplane with a single-place cockpit, powered by a 60-hp, six-cylinder Anzani (French) radial engine. On a visit to Archerfield, Charles Kingsford Smith flew the tiny plane and pronounced it "a very fine little machine" in the local press. Wikner himself claimed an Australian altitude record when he took the plane to 17,300 feet (5,273 m) in May 1931. George and Norm put two pairs of gloves on him, but he was half frozen on his return.

They built two more planes over the next two years—the Wicko Lion and the Wicko Wizard, both of which flew successfully. When Wikner decided to try his luck in England, he left the first plane with George and Norm, who stored it in Ipswich. They gave it to the Queensland Museum in 1982. Neither the Lion nor the Wizard survived, but Wikner went on to design and construct other successful aircraft in England.

When Arthur Baird moved to Brisbane, he began flying in aerial derbies. He had never stopped flying in Longreach, even though his job was mostly on the ground. By 1934, he had over 2500 flying hours, double that of Hudson Fysh, who was now hardly flying, because of his administrative duties. Fysh had been made manager in 1923.

Baird still enjoyed building, fixing and flying planes and there was an active community of enthusiasts in Brisbane. George thinks he and Norm first met Baird at an aerial derby. They would also see him at the new aerodrome at Archerfield, where Qantas moved its hangars in 1931. The Roberts boys were regular fixtures there, through their work with Geoff Wikner.

Still, they did not rush to ask Baird for a job. One reason is that during the Depression they knew there were no jobs to be had. Another was a sense of obligation to their father, running the service station. Another was that neither of them had any formal aircraft qualifications.

George: "It was virtually impossible to get your Ground Licences unless you worked for an airline. You could attend courses if you were apprenticed to an air company but we had already finished our apprenticeships."

In 1931, Britain's Imperial Airways mounted two experimental air mail flights to Australia.
In April, Qantas flew Australian mail to Darwin to connect with the service, using the DH61 Apollo,
piloted by Russell Tapp (third from left). Hudson Fysh is at far left. He piloted the second run to Darwin
and back in May. This got mail to London in 16 days, half the time it took by sea.

When the Depression eased slightly in 1934 Norm Roberts applied to join Qantas in the engineering department. George still has Arthur Baird's letter of acknowledgment to Norm, dated May 14, which says: "As you are not in a possession of any Ground Engineers' Licences you must realise it is going to be difficult to place you."

In fact, his application was well timed. Qantas was about to become an international airline, and for that, it would need staff.

A new era: the four-engine DH86 could fly over water, which allowed Qantas to become an international airline, but the water sometimes appeared where it wasn't expected. This is the landing ground at Daly Waters.

The ultimate prize in Australian aviation had long been the Imperial route, a mail and passenger service linking Australia and England across a map that was still largely coloured red, the hue of the British empire.

From 1931, the jockeying between the three major players in Australia to secure the leg to Singapore was intense. Brearley's WAA wanted a route via Wyndham; Smithy and Ulm's ANA wanted to extend their east coast services from Brisbane to Darwin and beyond. Failing that, since this was Qantas's backyard, they wanted the overseas part, where Qantas's single-engine aircraft could not operate. Hudson Fysh had forged strong links with Imperial Airways in England, hoping to link up with them at Singapore. The three Australian companies contemplated a merger, but talks failed in an atmosphere of mistrust. When tenders were called, Qantas and Imperial Airways Ltd (IAL) were successful with a joint bid, which would operate under a new joint company, Qantas Empire Airways Ltd (QEA).

Qantas ordered five new de Havilland 86 aircraft to fly the Singapore-Darwin leg. This British biplane with four Gipsy VI engines could take 10 passengers and mail. At 145 mph cruising speed, it was faster and bigger (with its 64¹/₂ foot wingspan) than anything Qantas had flown before.

Qantas won the tender three weeks before Baird's letter to Norm Roberts. Paul McGinness, then struggling to make a go of farming in Western Australia, sent a congratulatory telegram: "Congratulations your success in securing the contract. Best wishes your future." It was the future he had predicted in his farewell speech on the ground at Charleville 12 years earlier. Before another three years, McGinness lost the farm, walking out with nothing after ten years. "I was a fool to have ever left aviation, but we live and learn," he wrote in a letter to Edgar Johnston, head of the Civil Aviation Board. He was seeking a job, but Johnston could not help. He would eventually enlist in the RAAF when war came.

Norm Roberts joined Qantas in September 1934, a month before Lester Brain arrived from England, flying the first QEA DH86. Preparations were in full

Captain Lester Brain securing His Majesty's Air Mail in the DH61 for the inaugural service from Brisbane to Singapore in December 1934.
Qantas used the DH61 and the DH50J to carry the mail to Darwin, where it was transferred to Imperial Airways.

A DH86 undergoing service in the hangar at Archerfield. George joined Arthur Baird's team in 1936 and immediately took on responsibility for instruments and electrical components.

swing for the company's international debut two months later. Pilots were in training and the head office moved to larger premises in Creek Street, Brisbane. Norm entered a workshop readying itself for a new fleet. This task was hard enough but three disasters soon put a lot more strain on Baird and his department.

On October 3, 1934, a Qantas DH50J crashed on a scheduled mail run to Winton, killing the pilot and two passengers. On October 19, a new DH86 brought in by Holyman Airways, flying between Melbourne and Tasmania, disappeared in Bass Strait with nine passengers and two crew lost. Then on November 15, the second of Qantas's DH86s crashed before it could be delivered. The plane came down after leaving Longreach on the last leg of its flight from London, killing the four on board. The DH86 was immediately grounded for safety checks. For an airline trying to interest the public in its new imperial mail service, this was a cruel stroke, especially as the plane hadn't even made it into their hands.

In the end, Imperial Airways stepped in to cover the Singapore-Darwin Section so that the service could begin on schedule. Qantas used its existing DH61 and DH50J aircraft to fly to Darwin and bring the mail south. The DH86 was cleared to fly in late January. On February 26 1935, Captain G.U. (Scottie) Allan piloted the first ever Qantas overseas flight, from Darwin to Kupang in Timor, in the RMA *Canberra*. The RMA stood for Royal Mail Airliner. The 4360-mile (7016 km) Brisbane to Singapore journey took 3$^1/_2$ days.

Flying the Timor Sea: Captain G. U. (Scottie) Allan and first officer Bill Purton in the cockpit of a DH86 on the first international scheduled Qantas flight in February 1935. The instrument panel would become George's new best friend.

Iris and Pam (at left): The first DH50A made by Qantas in Longreach was christened Iris *on 18 August 1926. Pamela Brown-Beresford, the reverend's daughter, was there. George Dousha, Qantas engineer, is at far right.*

George Roberts finally joined Qantas in 1936. In the interview Arthur Baird initially told him he had no vacancy. "He also said 'We have never employed more than one person from one family. That has been a policy'.

"He then asked me: 'why should I employ you?'"

George asked him to look out the window at a low-slung Fronti Ford he had converted from "splash oil feed" to "pressure oil feed", a complex modification.

"He asked me what machinery I had used to do that? I told him I didn't have any because I didn't have the monies. I did it entirely by hand."

Baird then asked if there was someone who could recommend him, apart from his brother, who was by then stationed in Cloncurry. George asked him if he knew the Reverend James Brown-Beresford of Longreach?

Baird knew him quite well. George was engaged to his eldest daughter.

"You don't mean Pam?" asked Baird.

"Yes, I do," said George.

Arthur Baird had often taken her on test flights at Longreach when she was still a teenager. She became a nurse at Ipswich General Hospital and George met her at a hospital ball in the winter of 1931.

"I saw this lass and went and asked her for a dance. Next day I saw her walking on the other side of the street so I went over and talked to her. Later on she told me she knew right then that she was caught. We just seemed to click.

Pamela Brown-Beresford, on the dunes at Southport beach, circa 1936, before she became Mrs George Roberts.

"I don't know if that Longreach connection helped me get the job but I know Arthur Baird rang the reverend, because the following day, when Pam and I returned from a day at Southport, there was a message to ring Mr Baird.

"So I rang him and he said 'when can you start?' That's all he said. He was a man of very few words."

On Monday November 1, 1936, George Roberts started work at Archerfield with Qantas Empire Airways. He was 26 years old and right where he wanted to be.

"The day I started I said to Mr Baird, 'I have told you what I can do, but if I'm not satisfactory after a week or two, I'll leave. And if I feel I can't do my job, I'll come and tell you'."

Baird asked him what pay he expected.

"Whatever you pay initially," said George.

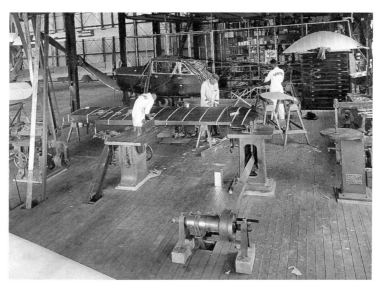

Near enough is not good enough: A section of the workshops at Archerfield in the early 1930s. A Qantas Puss Moth is having its airframe overhauled. "Mr Baird set very high standards," says George.

All night repairs: When a plane developed problems en route, maintenance crews often flew out from Brisbane. George, Norm and Mark Webber (right) worked well into the night to repair this DH86 in Longreach in 1937. "The heat was shocking," George remembers.

"Well it's £4 a week."

"All right, I accept that."

At the end of the first week, he went to see Baird again.

"Mr Baird, I've only been here a week but I know I can do this job for you and I reckon I can do the job quite well. I don't know what your thoughts are, but if I am satisfactory, then I need a rise."

"Why do you think you're satisfactory?" Baird asked him.

"Well you are having a lot of magneto trouble with the aircraft. With every flight up to Singapore and back, we've got magneto trouble each time. We have to change magnetos. And you are sending your instruments to Proud's Ltd in Sydney for overhaul. I can handle both of those things for you."

Baird gave him the rise, possibly the fastest in the history of Qantas.

"I went from £4 to £5 in one week. That was the start of the instrument overhaul and electrical overhaul section for Qantas. I had already been handling hundreds of them in the automotive business, almost exactly the same thing. Most of the instruments on the aircraft at that time, other than the gyroscopes, which I didn't have experience of, were all pressure or mechanical instruments and they were very similar to those on a motor car. I had taken on that work for our own business, in the garage."

A magneto supplies an electrical charge to the engine ignition. George soon solved the problem by replacing the platinum points in the magnetos with much tougher tungsten-iridium points and reducing the mechanical tolerances. In two years, he remembers that he converted about 1700 magnetos. "I was doing it for Qantas and all the people at the aerodrome as well."

He loved this work and did not find it repetitive. He had found his vocation in instruments. It was a specialty no one else in the airline had.

At the same time, both he and Norm studied for their Ground Engineer's licences. There were four basic types—A, B, C and D.

"A meant you were capable of overhauling the whole of the airframe; B meant you were capable of overhauling engines, and you would be licenced on one type of engine, then another type and so on; C meant you could do maintenance on the airframes; D meant you could do maintenance on the engines. A and B were the major licences. I had a licence on all four, as did Norm."

There were also specialist qualifications known as 'X' licences, on things like magnetos, propellers, welding and compasses.

"I had all of those too; that meant I could swing the compass and I was qualified to sign out the aircraft.

"When Norm joined Qantas there were 30 employees in total. When I joined two years later, there were 50, and 25 of those were in engineering."

That expansion came from the move into international operations with the five new DH86s, which had been designed specifically by de Havilland for Qantas's needs.

At Archerfield, the engineers worked under Arthur Baird's firm but fatherly care and supervision. There were no time clocks and no time sheets. Each person took responsibility for completing work as directed—even if it took half the night.

In Longreach, Baird had instituted a dual system for all work—one did the work, another checked it.

George: "His philosophy was always 'near enough is not good enough.' Everyone who worked under him remembers him always saying: 'Son, do you know what you're doing?' He was an engineer of exceptional ability."

Up until the arrival of the multiple engine DH86s, Baird would test fly most types of aircraft once they had been built or overhauled.

Baird also encouraged innovation. The engineers were there to improve the planes, not just keep them flying. For example, the DH86 could carry up to 10 passengers to Darwin, but only four could go on across the Timor Sea, because the plane had to carry extra fuel to make the 512-mile hop (824 kms). A special fuel tank had to be fitted in the cabin for each Timor flight. Qantas engineers solved the problem by designing a series of tanks that could fit into the undercarriage beneath the passengers' feet.

"Norm was the one who built those tanks and installed them, so that the aircraft could then take a full complement of passengers across the Timor Sea. Norm and I had learned how to weld non-ferrous metals before we joined Qantas, but not many people had that skill of welding aluminium and such. By building the tank into the aircraft itself, not only did they have the range, but also the weight of the fuel was below the fuselage so that the centre of gravity was much easier to control."

Archerfield was still only a grass field with no established runways and few services. There was no town sewage so passengers and staff alike used an outhouse situated across a road and down a well-worn path through the local cemetery.

The hangar could house two DH86s and a few smaller aircraft, but it was subject to Brisbane's extremely hot summers. George remembers a day when the mercury hit 44° Celsius inside the hangar and everything metal was hot to the touch. They were servicing a DH86, VH-USD, with the wheels removed and the plane supported by mobile jacks. First officer Fred Stevens was in the cockpit servicing the radio. Ken Butler, an engineer, notified Stevens that he was about to test the compression on all four engines. Butler made sure that all engine ignition switches were off and all four throttles were fully forward. In this position, the Gipsy VI engine was not supposed to be able to start, but one engine had an undiscovered fault in a magneto earthing lead. When Butler rotated the propeller of the port inboard engine, the engine coughed into life. The heat had vapourised enough fuel in the engine for the unearthed magneto to ignite it. On full throttle, the aircraft rolled forward on its jacks, demolishing a wooden trestle and sending a shower of splinters through the fuselage.

George: "An apprentice named Lance Loney tried to short circuit the engine by valiantly extending his bare arms across all six spark plugs, but he was thrown clear by the shock. Bill Stone, who was working on the airframe of another aircraft, tried to clamber over the trailing edge of the wing to get to the engine controls. The aircraft was now gathering speed and turning towards a store room.

"Arthur Baird, who was normally unflappable, appeared from within his office just when a catastrophe looked imminent, but the plane suddenly stopped. Fred Stevens had managed to extricate himself from a cramped position behind the captain's seat and close the throttle."

Though damage was slight, the crew worked all night so the aircraft could leave for Singapore next morning. It was the kind of freak accident caused by Australian extremes, which English aircraft designers working in a cooler climate would not be expected to anticipate.

A year before George joined Qantas, he and his brother embarked on yet another home-made aircraft. They had made three planes with Geoff Wikner, each of which flew, but none of their own had even had an engine.

In October 1935 the British publication *Newnes Practical Mechanics* published detailed plans for the Flying Flea, a tiny plane with a 13-foot wingspan designed and flown by a Frenchman, M. Mignet. The magazine described it as "probably the first practicable attempt to provide the man in the street with an easy and cheap means of learning to fly and of building his own aeroplane".

George: "It was a very unusual design. In most planes you have a joystick and a rudder

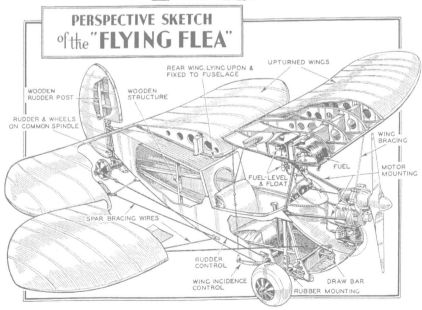

The Flea takes shape in the backyard in Ipswich. Norm in jovial stripes.

bar, but in this one there was only a joystick. It controlled both the rudder and the upper wing. The lower wing was fixed, but the upper wing was hinged, so you controlled the airflow by tilting the top wing."

The cost was quoted as £75 but George and Norm did it for less. The major expense was the engine, which George solved when he bought a Henderson motorbike engine for £3. They overhauled and modified it, hoping its meagre 11.5 hp would be enough.

Norm had become friendly with Dudley Wright, Arthur Baird's deputy in charge of maintenance. Wright was building a similar hobby plane, which he called the Wright Mite, but he had no engine. They agreed to share the engine between the two planes.

The Mite was the first to fly. Arthur Baird tried several times to get it aloft, but declared himself too heavy. A lighter pilot was successful.

Dudley Wright with the Wright Mite at Archerfield. The Roberts brothers shared their engine, which came from a Henderson motorcycle. The Mite was destroyed in a fire in Hangar No. 2 in 1939, along with six other aircraft.

The Flea had its debut in 1936, with Norm at the controls. Both brothers had by now earned private pilot's licences, but Norm took the lead, as he had done years before, jumping off the roof with their first glider.

Their friend Charles Matheson, who had been Qantas's first flying instructor at Longreach in 1926, urged Norm not to go up. They knew already that the engine was under-powered and there had been accidents with the Flea overseas. In the circumstances, Matheson was probably right—it was foolhardy. The Flea puttered off down the field, but it did not come unstuck from the ground until it reached a dip in the terrain.

"Charlie kept muttering to himself, 'keep it down, Norm, keep it down' as the plane climbed. Norm then circled the field several times, and brought the aircraft into a safe landing and taxied up to where we were standing. Charlie was very relieved and offered his congratulations."

The Flea was the first and only Roberts aeroplane which flew. In 1982, they donated it to the Queensland Museum. It now flies permanently, suspended over the main floor, above a carriage built by their grandfather and a fire engine built by their father.

The finished Flea. The Civil Aviation Department wrote to George and Norm
forbidding them to fly it. The aerodrome controller at Archerfield got the same letter.
"He told us we couldn't fly it there, but that he didn't start work till 9 a.m."
The plane now hangs in the Queensland Museum.

Do you, George Alexander Roberts? September 10, 1937, at Lutwyche, Brisbane.
Pamela's magnificent dress was made for her by two aunts, court dress-makers in London.

CHAPTER SIX

Water Wings and Wedding Bells

*T*he job with Qantas meant more than a career for George Roberts. It meant a new life.

The Depression had prevented his marriage, as it did thousands of young Australians. He and Pam had been courting for five years, but George had no money for a set of tools, let alone a wife. He was still living at home when he joined QEA. The £5 a week pay packet meant he could now get on with his life.

He and Pamela Brown-Beresford were married on September 10, 1937, at St Andrew's Anglican Church, Lutwyche, Brisbane. Her father was rector there and he married them, with Norm as best man and Bert Roberts playing the organ. George wore tails; Pam wore a magnificent dress made for her in London by two aunts who were court dress-makers.

"Customs charged me £10 when I went to collect it. Two week's wages," he remembers. (He gave the dress to his granddaughter Amie on her 18th birthday in October 2000. Right from birth she had been the spitting image of Pam.)

Dr Simmonds had predicted seven years earlier that he might marry when he was 28; in fact, he was three months short. As he had been at Qantas only ten months, he was not entitled to holiday leave, so the honeymoon was a weekend at Southport, a beach they both loved.

Southport 1938. From left, Honey, Pam and Ivy.

The newlyweds moved into a house in Dornoch Terrace, Highgate Hill, paying a steep rent of £1.17s.6d a week. They had a view of the city and the river. George says they were happy from the start. She had been his first real girlfriend and the only woman he had wanted to marry.

Norm Roberts had also been serious about a girl for some years. She was Ivy Cruickshank, though everyone called her Honey. They met through a gathering at St Paul's Anglican Church, Ipswich, where the Roberts family worshipped (and Bert Roberts played the organ for 60 years). When he returned from his posting to Cloncurry, Norm and Honey became engaged.

With money in their pockets, the brothers would sometimes hire a plane after work to go flying. Both had 'A' licences; to get a 'B' licence required 100 hours of flying. On December 9, 1937, they hired a Gipsy Moth after work, intending to go together. The plane, VH-UGW had once been a Qantas aircraft, but now belonged to Aircraft Pty Ltd at Archerfield. Public transport stopped four miles short of the aerodrome, so George's car was the link for four of his workmates. They were waiting as he swung the prop for his brother.

"I came round to get to the front cockpit, put my right leg in and then I said to Norm 'look, there are four people waiting for me to take them home. You go flying and we'll go flying again in the morning'.

"So I took the four people home, Norm took off and over the Brisbane River he went into a spin. He got out of the spin but hadn't got enough height to recover and dived into the river. The motor came right back into the cockpit, where I would have been.

"Fortunately, from Norm's point of view, the aircraft broke in two at the rear cockpit, which allowed him to get out, because he was wearing a harness. We looked at it afterwards and the harness in those days was fastened with a big split pin in the centre of your chest and that had bent right over. There was no way he could have released it under the water. He came to the surface of the river, swam over to one bank and then went up to a house there. The lady gave him a cup of tea. He got out of it with no broken bones, but the coincidence was that he hit the water very near the Indooroopilly Railway Bridge. The train going over held, of all people, his fiancee Honey and she saw this aircraft dive into the river and thought 'Gee, is that Norm?'

"So it was a very agitated girl who rode in that train from there through to East Ipswich. When she got there she ran up to our home to find out if it was Norm. My mother immediately said 'oh no, it can't be Norm, because

In his element: George at work on an altimeter in the Rose Bay workshops in 1939.

he only rang me 10 minutes ago and said don't keep dinner for me, because I've been detained in Brisbane for a while, and I'll be home late.' That's all Norm said on the phone, he didn't say anything about the crash.

"I knew nothing about this crash until one of our engineers knocked at my door. I can still see him, his name was Mark Webber, and he came to the door and he said: 'now George, don't get excited'."

"What have I got to be excited about, Mark?" asked George.

"Now please, don't lose your equilibrium."

"Has something happened to Norm?"

"Yes, yes, Norm's crashed into the Brisbane River."

"Is he all right?"

"Yes yes, he's all right, but we have got to go and collect him," said Webber.

By the time they got him to bed back at Ipswich, he was starting to shake.

"That went on and he got more and more shakes the next day, so on the third day, I felt, this is no good for him, so I collected him in the car, took him back to Archerfield, got another aircraft out and put Norm in it and said 'well, go on, you'd better go flying now'. He came down without the shakes. It took all the shakes away from him completely."

Norm thought he got out of the plane on the surface, when it broke in two.

"I said to him, 'no you didn't, you went to the bottom'. He said he didn't and I said 'yes, you did, you'd better look in the pocket of your jacket, it's full of stones'. He went 25 feet (7.6 metres) to the bottom."

The plane was a write-off but Norm's fiancee took it in her stride. They were married in 1939 at St Paul's in Ipswich.

Twelve days after the accident, the first Empire flying boat (named *Centaurus*) arrived from Britain on a route survey and propaganda tour. It landed on the Brisbane River, at Pinkenba, near Eagle Farm. People marveled at its size and elegance. There had been seaplanes and flying boats before—like the Curtiss Seagull—but nothing like this.

This engine and a pair of wheels is all that was left over after Norm put the Gipsy Moth into the Brisbane River in 1937.

George (right) and engineer George Williams take a first look at the Empire flying boat engine in December 1937. Centaurus alighted at Pinkenba, then taxied up river to the city reach for all to see.

Qantas was at the start of another major operational change, only three years after the last one.

Imperial Airways Ltd was planning the switch to flying boats two full years before the start of the joint London-Brisbane scheduled service in 1934. The plan was bold and very imperial: instead of charging the customer extra to send a letter by airmail, IAL wanted all first class mail to go by air throughout the British empire without surcharge. The vastly increased volume of mail would require bigger aircraft and increased frequency of services, which would benefit communications and passengers. It would strengthen links throughout the empire, not to mention's IAL's network and financial viability. The British and dominion governments would share the costs on a proportional basis, but the scheme could only work if it had the support of the whole empire. In the Australian government's eyes, this was far from assured.

The scheme was costly and it was born out of IAL's problems, which were not Australia's problems. The IAL fleet was aging and the mail surcharge system was not paying its way. In Australia, the QEA planes were new and airmail volumes since the start of the QEA service far exceeded expectations. The Australian government was in fact making enough money from the airmail surcharge to cover the subsidy to QEA. The IAL scheme would only cost money. It would also concentrate and centralise resources in IAL's hands. What would be the benefit for Australian aviation?

Nor would flying boats deliver much extra speed. The DH86 carried 10 passengers at 145 mph, although they were operating at more like 166 mph in QEA's hands. The Short Bros S23 Empire flying boat, when it was finished, would carry up to 15 passengers and five crew at 165 mph.

Qantas was in favour of the Empire mail scheme and the choice of aircraft. The DH86 was proving too small to cope with the volume of mail and still

*International services meant international visitors: Charles Chaplin, Paulette Goddard,
her mother and Qantas captain Russell Tapp on the tarmac at Batavia (Jakarta)
in 1936. Below: Noel Coward in tropical splendour on the steps of the DH86, 1936.*

carry passengers. The Australian government contract stipulated that mail must be given preference over passengers, so Qantas was missing out on a valuable source of revenue. Bigger aircraft would allow for carriage of both. (The problem was partly solved by doubling the DH86 service to run twice a week).

The biggest hurdle was political: Canberra saw the scheme as taking control of the route to Singapore out of Australian hands; the government of Joe Lyons refused to agree. The impasse was not resolved until 1937 and in Australia's favour. Through a separate contract with QEA, Australia would retain full responsibility for the service to Singapore; the

mail would still have a surcharge, though much reduced; the service could use flying boats, but either side could cancel the agreement before the 15-year expiry, if it felt it wasn't working.

This agreement was significant because it reinforced the idea of Australian sovereignty over Australian aviation, at a time when British capital still controlled large areas of Australian commerce and industry. Indeed, for Australia, the Empire Mail scheme was partly born by loosening the bonds of Empire.

For Qantas, this was a difficult step to take. McMaster and Fysh were both staunchly pro-British and Empire. The negotiations forced them into defining the limits of their loyalties to IAL. The deal was a reassertion that they were running an Australian airline, not a branch office of IAL.

One condition of the new scheme was that it would terminate in Sydney, not Brisbane. Another was that the six Australian flying boats would operate right through to London and vice versa. Australian crews would take them to Singapore and hand over to IAL crews. On the return to Australia, the Australian crew might fly a QEA or an IAL boat. Incredibly, the initial agreement also said all engine maintenance and repair was to be done in England, which would have had far-reaching, even devastating effects on Arthur Baird's engineering department. Hudson Fysh could see this would not work, nor was it in the spirit of maintaining Australian control. He was also strongly aware of the possibility of a European war. The idea was eventually dropped.

In late 1937, Arthur Baird and three of his deputies (Dudley Wright, Henry Williams and Eric Kydd) went to England with seven captains for training at Short Bros factory at Hythe, on the Solent, near Southampton.

When the *Centaurus* arrived in Brisbane in December 1937, Arthur Baird's team serviced it on the Brisbane River. It was the first plane to come in with an automatic pilot, but after leaving Marseilles under the command of IAL

Captain John Burgess, the bank and climb control unit of the instrument packed up. Arthur Baird asked George to see if he could "fix the thing".

"I had never seen one before in my life, so I took it to Archerfield, pulled the lid off it and looked inside and said to myself—where do I start?"

He soon discovered the problem, fixed it with ballbearings bought from the local bicycle shop and replaced it in the *Centaurus*. John Burgess cabled when he got back to London to say it worked perfectly all the way. Before he put it back, George noted the serial number of the B & C Control Unit and when the instrument next turned up in the workshop, he replaced it with a spare.

"Because it was the first automatic pilot into Australia, I felt we should retain that here."

The original stayed in Australia—in fact, George still has it. Along with a sense of history, he has always had a mania for collecting and preserving things—from spiders and beetles as a kid, to all his work notebooks, instrument manuals, tools and examples of the very instruments he worked on. Many of these now reside in the Qantas Historical Collection, which he helps to tend.

The move to flying boats pitched the airline into a period of intense activity and expansion. Bases had to be established around the north Australian coast for the service to Darwin and upgraded in the Dutch East Indies. Rose Bay in Sydney was to be

The bank and climb control unit of the first automatic pilot into Australia, from the Centaurus. George fixed it with bicycle ballbearings, and later made sure it stayed here. In aviation circles worldwide, the colloquial word for an auto pilot is always "George".

George and Pam set off for a new life in Sydney in a 1927 Model T Ford tourer,
the last sold by his father. George bought it back from the first owner.

the new base of operations, with a new company headquarters in the Shell
building in Margaret Street in the city. The old Brisbane-Darwin overland service
was discontinued but Qantas continued to fly DH86s to outback Queensland
and the Northern Territory, so the Archerfield hangars were retained. Most of
the staff transferred to Sydney in May and June of 1938, by flying boat. George
and Pam drove down in a 1927 Model T Ford tourer, the last sold by his father
before the model was discontinued. George had bought it back from the original
buyer. He and Pam were both excited by the prospect of living in Sydney.

The Commonwealth government was responsible for building a new
terminal, hangar and slipway at Rose Bay but only the terminal was finished
when they arrived.

George: "Rose Bay was chosen because it had the expanse of water,
the depth and because it was calm and close to the sea. It was by far the best

Qantas moves to Sydney—by hand. Norm (front)
and Dudley Wright load a filing cabinet on to the flying boat
Cooee, June 10, 1938.

place you could find here in Sydney. Initially, we had a number of huts built and we operated in those huts. I had a separate hut for instrument overhaul. They were corrugated iron Nissen huts. There was nothing else. When we went there, most of it was open space. The base was near Lyne Park, where the tennis courts are now. That was the maintenance headquarters and the terminal."

The first QEA Empire flying boat, VH-ABF *Cooee*, left Sydney a month later, on July 5, 1938, bound for Singapore and Southampton. Norm Roberts was on board, transferring to the QEA engineering base in Singapore. The route included overnight stops in Townsville and Darwin, Surabaya, Singapore, Bangkok, Calcutta, Karachi, Basra (Iraq), Athens, and Southampton, a distance of 12,847 miles (20,675 kms). The journey to Southampton took nine and a half days and cost £200, which for someone like George represented almost a year's wages. There was only one class—first.

The service ran three times a week, departing from Rose Bay at 7.30 a.m., usually on Monday, Wednesday and Friday.

Passengers had never traveled in such comfort. They sat in reclinable chairs in three cabins, with large windows, a separate observation deck and a smoking area at the back. The cabins were so spacious there was room to play mini golf on the observation deck (putters and balls were provided).

George: "Len Grey, who was then a first officer, used to set up the golf for the passengers. On one occasion when he was ready, he called to his Captain, Bert Hussey, and said 'hold the aircraft steady, we're putting'."

The flying boats had only one class—first. With a promenade deck and plenty of headroom, it was probably the most comfortable plane Qantas has ever flown and certainly the most romantic.

On a promotional flight in May 1938, VH-ABF Cooee dips gracefully over Brisbane.
The Storey bridge was still under construction.

Meals were sumptuous, with huge plates of oysters, full roast dinners, a choice of puddings and cheeses and a pay bar. The meals came on board in large vacuum flasks and wicker hampers and were served from a galley on fine monogrammed china. For the first time, Qantas put a steward on each flight, the first being Bill Drury, recruited from IAL to train local staff (all male at this stage). Refuse disposal was somewhat crude—the steward could open a window in the galley, because the plane, usually flying at below 10,000 feet, was not pressurised. Passengers brought warm clothes as a matter of course.

Forward of the passengers were two decks, the lower containing toilets, galley, purser's desk, lower mail storage and a mooring compartment in the nose. The pilot, first officer and radio operator were upstairs on a flight deck much bigger than any they had known. There were stowed beds which could be rigged up if a passenger wished to sleep, but these were rarely used since the planes mostly flew in daylight. What the passengers never knew was that they were sometimes sitting on top of a gold bullion shipment. The gold was transported in secret compartments beneath their feet. Going up, the cargo bay often held shipments of one-day-old chickens, destined for sale in the Singapore markets. Coming back, they often carried fresh seafood.

At Rose Bay, the slipway and hangar were not completed for over a year, which meant the boats could not be beached. All maintenance and overhaul had to be done on the water, including the changing of engines. Most of this was done at night when the water was calmest. The engineers stood on two platforms which hinged out from the leading edge of

*The highest mini-golf course
in the world.*

the wing, with a builder's plank slung between them, under the engine. The greatest danger was a dropped tool or engine part. These went to the bottom of the bay. The maintenance teams drilled holes in their tools and attached them to their belts with fishing line. If a large part such as an engine cowling fell into the water, a diver would be brought in to find it.

To test the calibration of the compasses, George had to lie down on the top of the flying boat, sighting along a row of rivets to fixed points on the harbour foreshore, while a boat rotated the aircraft through 360 degrees. This would be done just after dawn, to get good light and calm water.

After the engines and instruments had been serviced, they had to be tested in flight. George flew three times a week on these test flights, clambering around inside the aeroplane—even inside the wing cavities—to test his handiwork. "We used to fly directly over my house, so I would often wave to Pam."

The flying boats were the first all-metal aircraft that Qantas operated, and they dwarfed anything in the fleet. The wingspan was 114 feet (34.75 m), the length 88 feet (26.82 m). At maximum load, the aircraft weighed 40,500 pounds (18,370 kgs). The DH86, the largest plane Qantas owned before, had a maximum weight of 10,000 pounds (4,536 kgs).

The flying boat was powered by four 920-hp Bristol Pegasus X 'C' engines, which gave high performance and good fuel consumption, but required constant care and maintenance.

Once an engine was removed, it still had to be sent back to England for overhaul. By 1939, the Australian government agreed with the airline that the likelihood of a war in Europe made self-sufficiency essential.

Qantas began construction of an engine overhaul workshop in Vickers Avenue at Mascot. It was built in 39 days and ready for occupation by August 1939, two months before the Rose Bay hangar constructed by the government.

The view from the cockpit of a flying boat heading for Rose Bay in Sydney.

Flying boat flotilla, 1938: Maintenance crews at work on Champion *and* Calypso
on Rose Bay, with Coolangatta *behind.*

The elegant Rose Bay terminal, the only part of the flying boat base which was ready when Qantas moved to Sydney.

Air mail by sea. Before the war, each flying boat carried an average 1.3 tons of mail per flight, far more than had been possible with the DH86.

The slipway and hangars under construction in 1938.

Corio comes unstuck as it takes off for Singapore and London.
George took the picture from the mail launch (previous page).

Spanners on strings: before the slipway was completed, all maintenance took place on the water. To stop their spanners falling in the water, the engineers secured them to their belts with fishing line. Note the hoist above the engine and the work platforms slung below.

The all-metal flying boats were most vulnerable in the hull during take-off and landing. A piece of surface debris could punch a hole in the thin Alclad (duralumin coated with pure aluminium) sheeting of the fuselage and seawater, once inside the wing structure, was death to a flying boat. Before any take-off or landing, a yellow painted government launch would go out to clear a flight path and search for debris. George remembers that during the war, one flying boat hit the base of a large palm tree that was floating just below the surface.

The cockpit of a Short C-class S23 Empire flying boat. Only 32 were ever built, at Hythe in Southampton, to operate the ambitious Imperial Air Mail scheme. Captain Ashleigh Gay at the controls.

"The aircraft came in from a test flight, hit this stump, but didn't know they had hit it, because it sounded almost the same as hitting rough water. The engineer then opened the hatch to go down the ladder to the lower deck and immediately called to the captain, 'water below!' The captain gunned the engines and put the aircraft up behind the old Wintergarden Theatre, down there on the mudflat, but unfortunately the tide rose through it and ruined the aircraft. Once the salt water got into the airframe, which was duralumin alloy, there was no stopping it.

"We tried to save it by taking off the engines, the wings, the rudder and the fin, and we then took all the larger components out to the Nepean River at Wallacia (west of Sydney) and sank them all into the fresh water but it didn't stop the corrosion."

The aircraft were also susceptible to bad weather while moored. Before the service had run six months, QEA lost a flying boat when the *Coorong* broke from its mooring in Darwin harbour and was washed onto a rocky breakwater and pier. Norm Roberts was by now station engineer in Darwin. He had gone out to the *Coorong* early in the evening and started the engines to ease the strain. He was still struggling with the aircraft when it broke free about 8 p.m. and drifted ashore. It sustained serious hull damage and water penetrated the hull, but not the wing. They dismantled it and sent it back to Short Bros, where it was repaired and put back into service.

The loss came at a bad time for QEA, which was groaning under an avalanche of Christmas mail, beyond even the capacity of the 31 flying boats then in service across the Empire. On the England-Australia route, a total of 65 QEA and IAL aircraft, including land planes, flew over 1.1 million miles in five weeks to cope with the postal good cheer. "Nothing like it had ever been attempted before in air mail history," wrote Hudson Fysh.

George remembers a busy Christmas, because he was the sole instrument man at Rose Bay.

"I worked from Wednesday through to the Friday night, went home for four hours sleep, then went back on the Saturday. On the Wednesday, Christmas Day, Pam came down with some sandwiches and we ate them together in Lyne Park. That was our Christmas dinner."

Mooring a flying boat could be tricky. Captains had to learn how to sail the aircraft, using the engines, rudder and wind to get into position.

To calibrate the compasses, George would lie on the top, sighting along a
row of rivets as the aircraft was rotated through 360 degrees.

Arthur Baird's Rose Bay team in 1940, in front of a beached flying boat
with maintenance platforms in position. George is 13 from right, standing up.
Baird is second from right (with hat).

Qantas maintenance women working on a flying boat at Rose Bay in July 1944.
War gave women access to jobs they had never done before.

CHAPTER SEVEN

The Professor at War

gyroscope was a beautiful thing to George Roberts. He loved them as a boy, recognising that his bicycle wheel, spinning on its axis like the earth, was a form of gyro. As a man, he loved their intricacy, their precision and possibly the fact that he was one of the few people in the country in 1939 who understood them well enough to fix them. The more intricate and delicate the work, the more he liked it. He still has some of the syringes he used to oil the ballbearing races in the gyros. "You used two drops of oil only, and it was fish oil, because fish oil produces a meniscus. Other oils spread everywhere, which would throw the instrument off."

At Archerfield, he discovered that the gyros in Qantas aircraft were not being properly balanced, so a pilot could go off course. Having no manuals, he rigged up a crude 'jig' to fix the bench adjustment problems.

The flying boats came with Sperry gyroscopes, made by the Sperry Gyroscope Company of Long Island, New York. They had revolutionised flying in September 1929, when they introduced the Directional Gyro and the Sperry Horizon. These were the key to flying blind in cloud, where pilots had previously been vulnerable to sensory confusion. To quote from a 1936 Sperry manual, which George still has: "They made it possible, for the first time in the history of aviation, for the pilot to make steep turns, spirals and other manoeuvres in heavy clouds with an accurate knowledge of his flight attitude at all times and the ability to level off and come out on an exact course."

George: "Just before the war, Sperry sent a representative to Australia whose name was Pete Meyer. He set up at Essendon in Melbourne in a workshop allotted by Australian National Airways, and I went down to do one of the first courses he gave there. Pam came along too."

On September 3, 1939 Britain declared war on Germany. The Australian Prime Minister, Robert Menzies announced on radio that as a consequence, Australia was also at war.

"We were having dinner at a downstairs cafe in Collins Street with Pam's brother Tom when the announcement came that war had been declared. Tom was then studying for the church, but he immediately said: 'I'm going to join up.' We came up from the restaurant, walked along the street to an office there and he joined up on the spot."

A few days later, George and Pam sailed for Sydney on the *Manunda*, which was being converted to a hospital ship during the voyage. To their surprise, the ship turned right out of Port Phillip Bay, rather than left.

"We went right around Tasmania and took five days getting into Sydney, because they were already concerned about German U-boats in the area."

In fact, it would be Japanese submarines which would cause the most damage, eventually sinking 18 ships off the east coast of Australia and one off northern Australia for the loss of 605 lives. The largest disaster was from the sinking of the Australian hospital ship *Centaur* off Brisbane on 14 May 1943, with the loss of 268 lives.

George snapped this photo in 1940 at Rose Bay when a father brought his two children to see the mighty flying boats.

When war broke out, the Australian government impressed several flying boats and converted them to military use, changing their registrations. A18-11 was Calypso, which later crashed at Daru in Papua. Many Qantas air crews joined the Royal Australian Air Force. L to R, Flight Lieutenant Bill Purton, unknown, Flight Lieutenant Eric Simms.

Back in Sydney in late 1939, George tried to enlist, but was refused on the basis that his work constituted an essential service. The authorities were more right than they could have known. Over the next five years his knowledge of aircraft instruments and his ingenuity as an engineer would solve many problems, not just for Qantas, but for the Australian and American air forces fighting the Japanese. In terms of his career, these years would be the most gruelling, rewarding and exciting he would face.

The first immediate effect of the war for Qantas Empire Airways was that the Sydney to London service went from three times a week to twice. The surcharge on mail rose in an attempt to discourage volume. Several Qantas pilots, including the highly experienced Scottie Allan, joined the RAAF. The airline had flown six million miles since the start of the London run in 1934, without

*Qantas engineers overhaul a US Army Airforce B-24D Liberator bomber
in the half-completed Igloo hangar at Archerfield in 1943.*

injury to passengers or crew. It was making good profits too but the war
presented a very clear threat to its viability. If the London service stopped, how
would the airline continue? There were also commercial dangers, with KLM and
Pan-American Airways pressing for full access to Australian airports and
passengers. (KLM was already flying to Sydney, but without access to Australian
passengers or mail. Pan-Am was flying to Auckland.)

The London service was cut in mid-1940 when Italy joined the war
against Britain. QEA and the newly constituted British Overseas Airways
Corporation (combining Imperial Airways and British Airways)
immediately began a new 'horseshoe' service, with the 16 flying boats
remaining on the southern side of Italy when the Mediterranean route was
cut. They flew to India and Cairo, then south to Durban, where ships took the
mail to England.

The possibility that Japan would join the war was known well before the raid on Pearl Harbour in December 1941. The government made contingency plans as early as August for the return of flying boats to Australia if hostilities began with Japan. By October 1941 the government had taken over four Qantas flying boats with their full crews. Before the war was over, all of Qantas's fleet would be largely engaged in military flying.

At Rose Bay, George and his colleagues were increasingly occupied with overhaul and service of RAAF aircraft. They converted five flying boats to military use by the RAAF, fitting them with guns and bomb mounts and extra fuel tanks. They overhauled RAAF engines and instruments and trained RAAF engineers. Qantas had 290 employees at the outbreak of war and 409 by early 1941.

George was no longer the only instrument man. Harry Adby was the first to be recruited, then Ted Harper came over from Prouds Ltd and Brian Murton from Archerfield. George and Pam were now renting a house in Dover

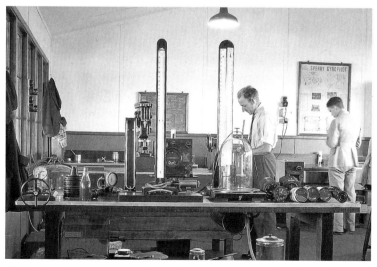

George at work in the vibration-free instrument workshop at Rose Bay in 1939.

A war time postcard commemorating the Japanese submarine raid on Sydney Harbour in May 1942. George remembers viewing the wreckage of the two subs on the harbour foreshore.

Heights, or Rose Bay East as it was then known, a short walk from the terminal. After Japan entered the war, many Dover Heights residents moved inland, fearing an attack. An air raid shelter was constructed in George's local park.

"As a girl, Pam had been in London in World War I. She'd seen bombs falling from the Zeppelins there, so she'd had that experience and it didn't worry her a bit. Neither of us ever went near the air raid shelter. Neither of us was concerned about it really. We didn't want to leave. We had work to do."

In fact, there were grounds for concern. At sunrise on February 18, 1942, two months after Pearl Harbour, a Japanese Yokosuka float plane launched from the submarine 1–25 flew over Sydney Harbour on a reconnaissance, apparently undetected. The pilot was Warrant officer Nobuo Fujita. He flew over Sydney again on May 23, eight days before the three midget submarines entered Sydney Harbour. One attacked the cruiser *USS Chicago*, missing it and killing 19 sailors on the *Kuttabul*, a converted ferry being used as a barrack ship. One of the subs made it out of the harbour but the other two were sunk. George remembers hearing the depth charges launched by naval patrols hunting them. The wreckage of the subs was later displayed on the harbour foreshore, then toured around the country, to Adelaide and back. Another float plane piloted by 2nd Lieut. Susumu Ito made similar forays on May 30, 1942 and January 25/26, 1943. The next evening, a Japanese submarine off Bondi shelled Rose Bay in an attempt to destroy the flying boats and their base.

George and Pam heard the shells coming over their house.

George's domain: in 1942 the instrument overhaul section moved into a converted bus depot at Double Bay. In the next three years they would process an unprecedented number of instruments.

"I ran up the road to the cliffs and I could see them being fired from the sea. I couldn't see the submarine but I could see they were coming from water level, so I knew it had to be a submarine, not a surface vessel. I could see them falling into the water at Rose Bay. Others fell on the land, some in Manion Avenue, some in O'Sullivan Road. Mostly they didn't explode, but one fell in a block of flats, piercing two walls in one flat and coming to rest on the stairs outside. The occupant tripped over the shell trying to get out and it rolled down the stairs and he rolled down with it, breaking his leg, but it still didn't explode."

None of the shells hit a flying boat, nor the Qantas base.

George's instrument overhaul section grew rapidly once the Japanese entered the war. In early 1942, with 30 people, the section moved to a converted bus depot at the corner of Bay and Cooper Streets, Double Bay. George's war then began in earnest.

Aircraft instruments began coming in by the thousands, mainly from the US Air Force and Navy fighting in the Pacific, but also the RAF, the Royal New Zealand Air Force, and the French and Dutch airforces. George had four main problems—not enough machinery, not enough skilled workers, not enough parts and not enough time.

The workforce problem was partly solved by the Department of Aircraft Production (DAP) "manpowering" every available watchmaker and skilled jeweller in Sydney. They were trained and set to work on altimeters, airspeed indicators and rate-of-climb indicators; all delicate instruments similar to clocks and watches. About 30 local women from nearby suburbs were trained to work on an instrument overhaul production line. Significant numbers of women were also working on engine overhaul at Rose Bay, Mascot and Randwick.

George trained many air force engineers on gyroscopic instruments.
At left, they test an autopilot on the original Scorsby. At right, the same
instrument after George modified it to test multiple instruments.

One job done almost exclusively by the women was instrument dial-painting. In a separate "luminising room", two shifts of four women painted aircraft dials with a special and highly toxic radium compound known as 22M. Each woman worked on a special desk, looking through lead glass, wearing a rubberised lead apron over a protective gown and medical gloves. After a shift the women washed in water that was collected in drums, not let into the sewer. As they left, they walked through a darkened room, where any speck on their clothes and hands would show up under ultraviolet light. George remembers they deliberately did not employ anyone with artistic training. "They had a habit of pointing their brush by putting it between their lips and that would have been disastrous."

Later they changed to a non-toxic compound because the 22M was so luminous, enemy pilots could see the cockpits glowing in the dark. The instrument section eventually grew to 187 people, working six days a week, but the problems of machinery and parts remained. Both of these required all of his ingenuity to solve.

Automatic pilots, directional gyros and artificial horizons were tested on a Scorsby, a complex instrument built by Qantas from a Sperry design, but it couldn't keep up. The Americans were flying whole planeloads of instruments into Mascot by C54 transport (the military version of a Douglas DC4), requiring them to be turned around at great speed. (Where they came from was secret, but George says they sometimes knew the code names attached to each instrument. "White poppy" was the battle for Guadalcanal in the Solomons, for example.) George modified the Scorsby so that it could test two auto pilots and 12 blind flying instruments simultaneously, increasing its output by a factor of 13. They doubled that by building a second Scorsby.

Once overhauled there was the problem of how to get the extremely sensitive instruments back to the lines.

"We had four-gallon steel drums made by Rheem, the water heater people, with a lid that could be locked on very solidly. Then we tried various materials inside, like sponge rubber, but that was unsuitable. We went eventually to horse hair covered in latex and that absorbed all the shock. In fact, we tested it by dropping it five floors in a building and bowling it down a set of stairs, and it worked very satisfactorily."

The Imperial route was cut completely once Japan took Singapore in February 1942. From then till the end of the war, Qantas was increasingly functioning as an arm of the military, but without some of the privileges of uniform, nor some of the restrictions. It was fortunate that people like George could also think militarily. He had been seven years as a reservist in the AIF First Cavalry Field Ambulance before the war. He solved the problem of a lack of spare parts from the RAAF's aircraft stores by using a trojan horse.

Every gyroscope was fitted with six ballbearing races which had often to be changed. They were made only in the US and each time George asked the

DAP for spares he got the same reply: 'nil stocks'. There were two main RAAF stores, one at Dubbo, another at Drayton near Toowoomba. As a civilian, he was not allowed into either.

"We were repairing their instruments and the RAAF'S own Aircraft Inspection Department was sharing our premises at Double Bay. Their inspectors checked to make sure what we had done was serviceable.

"When I could not get permission to go into No 6 Stores depot in Dubbo I approached the Aircraft Inspection Department here, because they had an inspection department in Dubbo as well. What we did was, we calibrated six gyroscopes here and then after they were inspected, we immediately decalibrated them, so that when they were inspected by AID in Dubbo, it would cause an inquiry. That is how I got into Dubbo."

The Commanding Officer at Dubbo was Group Captain Tex Rickhard, whom George had known in Sydney, through Jones and Rickhard Engineering.

"What are you doing here, George?" asked Rickhard.

"Tex, I haven't been able to get in here to get any spares."

George explained that Dubbo might have parts they could not identify. Rickhard arranged immediate access. "His words to the Squadron Leader in charge of G Group stores were: 'Get this man anything he wants, and let him see what we've got'."

Inside the enormous igloo-shaped stores building, George went to work. In one huge crate he found precious exhaust gas analysers.

"There were seven Lockheed Hudsons sitting grounded at Bankstown because we didn't have the parts to service their exhaust gas analysers. I explained this to Tex and he arranged for them to be taken immediately to the railway and sent down to my people, who took them straight to Bankstown".

George also discovered 14,000 bearing races, enough to fix thousands of gyroscopes. "These didn't last very long so my next move was to No. 7 depot at Drayton and I did the same thing and came up with another 14,000. That kept us rolling, but in fact, we just got through."

It would be hard to overstate the importance of this work to the war pilots. Without blind flying gear and auto pilots, they would have had to severely restrict the conditions they could fly in or take much greater risks.

Aside from the watchmakers and jewellers, George found local engineering businesses to make parts and tools which couldn't be got from overseas. One of these was a Mr Podmore, of the Silvarite Glass Company in Broadway.

"In a pressure instrument, you needed a laminated piece of glass that you could see through, in other words two pieces of glass glued together, but the whole thickness could only be one sixteenth of an inch. It was laminated so if one piece of glass cracked, the instrument was still pressurised. Apart from making the lenses our problem was finding the right material to use as glue. Podmore had contacts at Sydney University and through them, he discovered it was balsam that they were using overseas. He made thousands and thousands of lenses for us. The experience that man had with glass was phenomenal."

Some problems George was able to solve himself. The flying boat engines used an electrical starting coil made by the C.A.V. company in England. When supplies dried up, George discovered that the starting coil of a Model T Ford did the job and these were in plentiful supply. "In fact they worked better than the original coils. We used those throughout the war."

Running a section with 187 staff took him away from hands-on maintenance work for the first time in his career. There were problems he had never encountered, nor even expected.

"Ted Harper, who was my assistant, came into the office one day and told me he had a problem with Mrs so and so."

"She's come into work this morning in the shortest shorts you could possibly put on and a see-through blouse and it's upsetting the whole workshop," said Harper.

"Well Ted, what have you done about it?" asked George.

"I can't, I can't do anything about it," replied a deeply flustered Harper.

George called the woman in, explained that her undress was inappropriate and gave her time to go home and change.

"I'm staying as I am," she replied.

George asked her to go back to work and consider her response.

"I'll give you ten minutes to make up your mind, then I'll take action."

The interval did nothing to defuse the stand-off.

"I'm staying where I am," she said.

"Well, if you're going to act like a child, I'm going to treat you like a child," said George. He swung her across his knee and gave her "one great belt across the bottom". Red-faced, the woman went home and changed.

"The alternative was to sack her and I didn't want to lose her. She was a very good worker. Today, I know I wouldn't get away with it."

The women were a diverse group and George says there were very few problems integrating a male and female workforce. "These women wanted to work. We all geared up until we were virtually working round the clock. We were running an instrument school there too, for the services, so we had people coming from the RAAF, the RAF, some from New Zealand, and also the Dutch and French. We taught them how to service and overhaul their gyroscopic instruments."

George had never worked so hard in his life, nor had the work ever been so rewarding. "The hours were exceptional, but it really was an exciting time."

It was during this time that he earned his nickname. His friend E. Bennett-Bremner, QEA's publicity officer, dubbed him "the professor", a title that must have pleased him. Arthur Baird was also pleased with his results. At a party, he told Mrs Roberts: "You know that man of yours, he had a go at me this week. He really ticked me off, but you know, I can't get rid of him, because anything I give him, he can do'."

The idea of George raising his voice to a man he so respected (at 90 he stills calls him "Mr Baird") is a surprise. "The cross words we had, I wish we'd never had, that's how much I thought of the man."

George admits he had a temper sometimes. "I would say yes, I could have. Even as a kid, my brother Norm would get into fights, but I always finished them."

By then, Norm was getting into fights that neither of them could finish. From 1940 he was back in Darwin as station engineer, when the war came to him. Before Singapore fell, QEA had withdrawn its base to Batavia (Jakarta) in Java. The flying boats played cat-and-mouse with Japanese fighters, often putting down in sheltered bays and hiding under trees till the coast was clear. As the Japanese advanced into the Dutch East Indies, the QEA base was withdrawn again, to Tjilatjap on Java's west coast, from where the flying boats evacuated 88 refugees and tons of cargo to Broome, the closest Australian port.

The flying boat numbers were already dwindling. *Corio* was shot down on 30 January 1942, approaching the Timor coast, with the loss of ten passengers and three crew (five survived, including Captain A. A. Koch).

Corinthian and *Circe* were the last to leave Tjilatjap on February 28, but *Circe* never made it home. No trace was ever found.

In Darwin, most of the wives and children of Qantas personnel had been evacuated by mid-February 1942, but Honey Roberts did not want to leave her new husband. She was still there when 188 Japanese planes attacked Darwin on February 19, just four days after the fall of Singapore.

Norm Roberts' own account of the raid says there were 24 QEA people in Darwin at the time, including two crews about to take the flying boat *Camilla* to Broome to help with evacuation from Java. *Camilla* was moored about 180 metres from the wharf. With five others, Norm had gone to collect charts and equipment from her in the Qantas launch *Naiad*. They were returning when "suddenly the sea before us went up in a mighty roar". Going ashore was more

Norm Roberts and Earl Bedell servicing a flying boat engine on the Brisbane River. Norm was station engineer in Darwin and chief engineer in Perth for the secret Indian Ocean service from 1943.

Darwin burns after the Japanese air raid of February 1942. At centre, the Neptuna and Barossa burn. At far right, the flying boat Camilla is just visible, protected by the pall of smoke.

dangerous so they turned the *Naiad* out into the open bay, but its engine failed about 800 metres from shore.

"The trouble proved to be water in the petrol but as the engine was hot we worked with great difficulty removing the carburettor. While we were working on the engine, the fast running-out tide carried us into the midst of the shipping and we could see that the *British Motorist*, an oil tanker, had begun to settle and was heeling over. Other ships were on fire. The aerial activity had now intensified considerably with the arrival of a swarm of Zeros."

As they got the *Naiad* moving, one Zero came after them. "We dropped speed immediately to foil his aim—his bullets went over our heads." Another Zero attacked them as they beached the Naiad in mangroves. They used branches shorn off by the bullets to camouflage the boat. They could see two more ships on fire at the wharf, the *Neptuna* and the *Barossa*, and the American destroyer *Peary* under intense attack. "The end of the *Peary* came in one great explosion and the ship was engulfed in flame and smoke. We had a

The Qantas hangar in Darwin after the air raid.

final glimpse of the stern going down but when the smoke cleared, there wasn't anything of the ship in sight."

When the raid was over, they ran the *Naiad* back across the bay to refuel and attempt to tow the *Camilla* away from the burning *Neptuna*. As they got to the flying boat base, the *Neptuna* exploded, showering them with debris and flame. "Until this event, the QEA building had escaped with only a few bullet holes, but then it just burst apart."

Camilla was now taking off, with Captains Bill Crowther and Bert Hussey to the rescue. The Qantas hangar was also largely destroyed. Norm souvenired a twisted lump of metal, which George still has. Honey Roberts had survived intact and she flew out that night on a flying boat which came in from Broome. She was the last woman to leave Darwin.

Norm's account does not mention that he also took a dinghy out into the bay to help rescue the many people who had jumped or been blown off the ships. The dinghy was powered by an outboard he and George had made from a motorcycle engine.

"Norm had taken this to Darwin with him and he installed that on a dinghy because the launch was out of action. He realised that he could not pick up people in the dinghy so he put ropes around the edge and towed people back to shore. He did this a number of times. Because of the history of that little engine, we donated it to the Queensland Museum."

Coincidentally, the only ship left afloat after the raid was the hospital ship *Manunda*, the one George and Pam took back from Melbourne in 1939.

Two weeks after Darwin, the Japanese launched a devastating attack on Broome, sinking 16 flying boats at their moorings. Two of these were QEA aircraft, *Corinna* and *Corinthian*. Most of the rest were Dutch flying boats. None of the QEA staff was killed, but several RAAF personnel and Dutch women and

The Waratah motorcycle engine cum plucky outboard.

Qantas Catalina base at Nedlands, Perth, circa 1944. Norm is at far right in uniform. He established the maintenance base.

children evacuees were. QEA now had to abandon Broome as a base, though Darwin remained open, despite the raid.

In July 1943, Qantas embarked on a remarkably bold new route—a secret service across the Indian Ocean from Perth to Ceylon, flying non-stop in Catalinas, American flying boats built for long-range reconnaissance. Norm Roberts was sent as station engineer to establish a base on the Swan River. He arrived with 50 spark plugs bought en route in Melbourne. That was the extent of his spare parts. There was an American Catalina base nearby, where he sometimes went to scrounge tools. He paid for these loans with carved ebony elephants brought back from Ceylon.

This was the longest non-stop air route in the world at the time and completely secret: 3513 miles (5654 kms) in radio silence, in a journey that took up to 32 hours. The service ferried essential mails and priority passengers to link up with BOAC's scheduled service to Durban, via Karachi. In the next three years, Qantas made over 800 crossings, flying 4.4 million miles, undetected by the Japanese. The service was eventually dubbed the Kangaroo route and those who flew on it got a certificate stating that they were members of the 'Secret Order of the Double Sunrise', so-named because the flight passed through two dawns.

For Qantas, the Indian Ocean service was a godsend: it got them back into international scheduled services, even if they couldn't tell anybody about it. The war was not going to last forever; nor would it be the same world afterwards. Qantas had almost ceased to exist as a commercial airline during these dark years, but the Indian Ocean service revived its spirits.

A Catalina approaching Koggala Lake, Ceylon, on the longest non-stop air route in the world, the secret Indian Ocean service begun in 1943.

The last of the great S-23 empire flying boats. Coriolanus made it through the war only to be scrapped at Rose Bay in 1947. George tried in vain to buy it.

CHAPTER EIGHT

Kangaroos Might Fly

antas finished the war with only one Empire flying boat intact, *Coriolanus*. The others died in various parts in various ways. *Corio* was shot down and *Circe* probably was; *Corinna* and *Centaurus* were destroyed at Broome; *Coolangatta* and *Clifton* were destroyed in accidents alighting at Rose Bay; *Coogee* and *Corinthian* suffered similar fates at Townsville and Darwin respectively. *Calypso* crashed at Daru in Papua. *Camilla* crashed in bad weather off Port Moresby, piloted by Captain A. A. Koch, who had survived the shooting down of *Corio*. In this second crash, on April 22, 1943, 11 passengers and two crew were lost, but Koch and first officer S.W. Peak survived by swimming for 18 hours. Some of these aircraft were in the hands of RAAF crews; some were Qantas Empire Airways crews. Most were flying on wartime duties.

Carpentaria, Coorong and *Cooee,* three of the original QEA six, actually made it through the war, but on the London side, operating as BOAC aircraft, only to be scrapped in 1947 at Short Brothers factory in Hythe, from whence they came.

George Roberts finished the war more happily, with a great sense of achievement. His logbooks showed his staff had processed 143,000 aircraft instruments since 1939, an extraordinary tally. More than that, he and Pam had also produced two sons.

"We had been waiting for a number of years before they came. In fact Pam had had some tests because we were concerned initially that no children had arrived."

The first was born April 17, 1943 at a private hospital in Rose Bay. "The sister there was Joan Brown. She had been a nurse with Pam in Queensland, and when I brought Pam in, Brownie said 'George, get out, you're not wanted', so I bolted. I waited at home for the news."

Bruce Llewellyn Roberts was born just before midnight. George distributed cigars at work the next day. Six months later he took his new family to Brisbane on the flying boat.

"The captain, Orm Denny asked me to bring the baby up and put him in his lap, so that later he could say he was in the pilot's seat at six months of age."

Sixteen months after the first child, Rodney Thomas Roberts was born, almost the same interval as between George and Norm. The new arrivals came at the height of George's war, so he didn't see as much of them as he would have liked.

The war ended in Europe in May 1945 but dragged on until August in the Pacific. "I was at work at Double Bay when we heard on the wireless that the war was over".

Fatherhood: George with Rodney and Bruce (right) and the 1928 Delage DM in Centennial Park, Sydney, just after the war.

The F/N with Bruce and Rod at Ipswich, taken in September 1952.

After the war, Qantas was short of aircraft, but not short of new routes. A number of ex-RAAF Catalinas flew on new services to Papua and New Guinea and Pacific islands.

The Australian government had already decided that Qantas would continue to be Australia's overseas airline after war's end: the question was, with what? In mid-1944, Britain allocated two converted Liberator bombers to the Kangaroo route, flying a shorter route via the Exmouth Gulf. The Catalinas continued to fly from Perth, until July 1945. Three DC3s provided by the Australian government were running a service between Sydney and Lae in New Guinea, but QEA desperately needed aircraft to reopen the Sydney-London service. Some of the aircraft QEA was using—including the Catalinas—either had now to be paid for or destroyed, under the terms of wartime lend-lease agreements. After doing heroic duty across the Indian Ocean, four of the Catalinas were flown out to Rottnest Island and sunk. Several more were chopped up with axes at the Rose Bay terminal. For people like George and his brother Norm, watching aeroplanes end this way was heartbreaking, but there was nothing they could do.

George actually tried to buy *Coriolanus* in 1947, but the company would not sell her to him. He planned to tow it up the Parramatta River, beach it and turn it into a garage on a block of land he leased at Parramatta. Instead, the last of the Empire flying boats, perhaps the most elegant and romantic plane Qantas ever flew, was scrapped at Rose Bay. Arthur Baird gave one of its propellers to the Rose Bay RSL Club, which now occupies part of the old flying base site. It hangs inside the building, the last sign of the base and the flying boats which flew from there.

The end of the war meant the end of wartime supply lines for spare parts, but not the end of demand. George's team dropped in number, as most of the women gave up their jobs, but the Instrument Overhaul Section was still busy on RAAF aeroplanes and work from outside Qantas.

"There were very large shortages initially and that went on for two or three years."

The London-Sydney service reopened in June 1945, flying converted Lancaster bombers, now called Lancastrians. The route was through Learmonth in WA, Ratmalana in Ceylon, then Karachi, Lydda (Palestine) to Hurn in southern England. The Lancastrians could cruise at 230 mph and carry nine passengers but they were only intended as a stop-gap until British aviation could produce a passenger aircraft to rival what American companies like Lockheed were already doing with their new pressurised aircraft, the Constellation.

The Lancastrians made the Perth-Ceylon Catalina service redundant, but George had no spare parts for the "Lancs". In particular, he needed DR (Distant Reading) Master compasses and generators for the RPM indicators, which were seizing up on the long flights to Australia. "Operating over Germany was quite a different thing to flying 100 hours to Australia and back.

"His solution was highly creative, highly irregular and highly risky.

Lancaster bombers were converted for civil use and called Lancastrians.
They carried up to nine passengers and air mail on the Kangaroo route to London
and a new service to Japan.

There were two Royal Navy aircraft carriers berthed at Pyrmont, *HMS Pegasus* and *HMS Pioneer*. Before returning to England, they were to dispose of 776 surplus aircraft at sea—more victims of lend-lease arrangements. George knew that these aircraft had the instruments he needed to keep the Lancastrians flying.

"I went to see the man in charge of the docks at Pyrmont, Commander Hines, a Royal Navy chap, and explained our problem. He told me I could take what I needed while the aircraft were still on the docks, but once they were loaded on the carriers they were under the control of the captains. The captain of the *Pioneer* would not have anything to do with it at all, but the captain of

the *Pegasus* could see the logic of getting the spares."

George then went to see the local police, to explain what he was doing. "I asked them if there was anything they wanted. They said 'yes, we want the gun cameras'. I said, 'okay, I'll get you the gun cameras if you leave me alone'."

George told Arthur Baird what he was doing but they agreed not to involve anyone else, so George set to work alone, starting with the aircraft on the docks. This was a huge job. There were 720 Grumman Avenger III torpedo bombers, 32 Grumman F6F Hellcat fighters, and 24 Fairey Barracudas, an English torpedo bomber. He doesn't remember how many instruments he liberated, but he kept at it for some weeks.

"I got all 24 DR master compasses from the Barracudas, and I remember taking 70 artificial horizons and 70 directional gyros in one day. I often went out to sea on the *Pegasus*, because there wasn't sufficient time to get the parts out on the wharf. On one occasion I was still working on an Avenger III when they said 'come on, George, get out of there, we're dumping

A Liberator bomber does civilian service at Mascot, just after the war.

this one over the side now'."

Most of the aircraft were new. "They were still embalmed, with protective insulation on them." The dumping site was off Gosford. For years, he remembers hearing reports of fishermen catching their nets on the sunken aeroplanes.

"One day I was on the wharf and just about to get out of a plane with some instruments when a gun was poked into my stomach. I was then marched onto the *Pioneer*, to the Sergeant-at-Arms. I told him I was working under the authority of Commander Hines, and he said: 'That is nothing to do with me'. So he called the police and put me in the brig for half an hour, but the police didn't come. He tried phoning the police again but they still didn't come, so they marched me off the ship and released me. I was driving out of the gate in my car as the police finally arrived and I waved to them and they waved to me."

Many of the parts eventually found their way to England as replacements on the Lancastrians. Other parts came from disposal auctions around the country. At Archerfield, George paid £50 for a small hill of parts, took out what he wanted then sold the rest as scrap, again for £50. Complete serviceable aircraft were going for ridiculous prices—a Spitfire could be got for £10. "Somebody bought a DC3 for £50".

The post-war aviation world was very different. Britain was well behind American technology in large aircraft. Australia's civil fleet was well below what it had been in 1939 and the Labour government of Ben Chifley wanted to nationalise the airlines.

Qantas still favoured British aircraft, but tests on those being offered proved unsatisfactory. Against stiff British opposition, Qantas decided to buy the Lockheed Constellation, the prototype of which Hudson Fysh had flown on during a visit to Lockheed in January 1945.

The flying Kangaroo: George's unique photograph was almost ruined by a Hollywood photo lab.

That decision meant George was to spend most of 1947 in America. He left Australia in February 1947 on a DC4, on a new service flown by a new joint Australian-British-New Zealand company, British Commonwealth Pacific Airlines. This was his first flight across the Pacific. Sir Frank Packer, the newspaper magnate, was also on board, as was the first kangaroo to be transported to the US by air, headed for Toronto Zoo.

"About an hour out of San Francisco, at 10,000 feet, the captain let it out of the hold and it bounced up through the cabin. I got out of my seat, which was on the starboard side and it bounced on to my seat and I quickly took a picture of it. Frank Packer said to me: 'George, that photograph is worth a mint'. He gave me the addresses for a lot of newspapers in America and Canada that he would be visiting and told me to send them a copy of the photograph and to charge each of them £200."

George couldn't believe his luck. Unfortunately, the photo lab in Hollywood ruined the film, so he could only salvage a bad grainy print of the first flying kangaroo, looking somewhat plaintively out the window of the DC4. The photo is reproduced here for the first time.

The same kangaroo is welcomed to Oakland airport, February 1947.

George's first stop in the US was the giant Lockheed plant at Burbank, near Hollywood. He could hardly believe his eyes—they had a regular bus service to take the employees around the vast facility.

The Constellation had been in development for some years at the request of Howard Hughes. Hughes was many things— heir to a petroleum fortune, movie producer, owner of a large portion of Transcontinental and Western Airlines (TWA), but perhaps most of all, an aviator. Before the war, he had asked Lockheed to build him an aircraft that could fly non-stop from the west to the east coast of America, with a 6000-pound payload at 300 mph (483 kph). The first model, designated the Lockheed 49, could carry 64 passengers, a major advance in civil aviation. The modern era of mass passenger transit was beginning.

Qantas ordered the later L749 model, because of its longer range. The passenger limit of 38 plus 10 crew was still well ahead of anything they had flown before. The "Connie" could cruise at 318 mph (511 kph) at 20,000 feet (6096 m) and had a range of 4800 miles (7,720 kms). The engineering was also much more complex, including the instruments. George spent most of his time on the east coast, because many of the components were being made there.

The L749 Constellation – built by Lockheed at Burbank, California.
The "Connie" revolutionised post-war air travel with its pressurised cabin and long range.
Qantas was among the first to buy it.

Norm was with him for part of the time, staying at the same hotel in Manhattan. Brian Murton and electrician Jack Ray joined him later in Paterson, New Jersey, to study new instruments at the Eclipse Pioneer plant, a division of Bendix International, at Teterboro airport.

"All of the instrumentation after the war was almost totally different. Before the war, most of the instruments were mechanical and pressure types. The readings on the latter came from variations in the pressure within the instrument. After the war, most instruments became electronic and that developed from research during the war."

American dogs must have been relieved at these breakthroughs. Before the war, the Sperry Automatic Pilot used dog skin as a membrane across its three pneumatic valves, because dog skin is exceptionally flexible but non-porous, which allowed the pressure on both sides of the valve to be maintained accurately. Post-war electronics superseded dog-skin diaphragms.

America was an eye-opener for George. It was his first long stay away from Australia and there were many cultural surprises, for both sides. "Going over there, we took with us tea and a teapot and also Vegemite, because there was nowhere to buy it and they didn't know how to make a cup of tea."

On one weekend, the three Qantas men decided to go to the beach at nearby Asbury Park. A policeman stopped them as they walked out of their hotel in Paterson.

"Sir, you're not allowed on the sidewalk in shorts," said the policeman. Dumbfounded, they pointed to a man wearing shorts in his front garden.

"He's on his own property, not the sidewalk," said the policeman.

At the beach, they were perplexed to see a series of poles in the water, with connecting ropes.

"We decided this must be where people learned to swim so we swam out beside the poles and did a little surfing and then set off back towards the beach. Just as we stood up Jack Ray, who was in the centre of us, was pushed under water by the chief lifeguard, and naturally, Brian and I, we pushed him under water. He went down and came up spluttering and we didn't know what all this was about until another fellow came running along the beach and he asked us 'Are you fellas Australians?'

"Of course by this time, we had a very, very irate lifeguard, but anyway, he cooled down after a time and he told us the poles were a safety measure, because very few Americans could swim. We had committed the sin of swimming out to get a wave. The other fellow had been to Australia during the war and he guessed we must be Australians because we went out surfing."

They weren't surprised that the Americans did not know much about Australia; they were surprised when they got questions about California. "On the east coast, I was asked so many times 'what's the west coast like?'."

One problem with gyroscopic instruments made in the USA was that they needed recalibrating for operation in the southern hemisphere. "I was talking to one of the top men at Bendix International about this problem and asked him why they couldn't calibrate them on the equator, which would then allow it to be correct for both northern and southern hemispheres and he said 'oh, no difference'.

"I said 'of course it's different, it's like the water going down the sink. Here the water goes down clockwise, but where we are it's anti-clockwise'. He thought I was pulling his leg."

At Teterboro, Eclipse Pioneeer was testing their new PB-10 automatic pilots on a B25 Mitchell bomber, which was equipped for fully automatic flying. George flew on it several times.

"All the pilot did to take off was push the throttles forward and the aircraft did the rest. The instruments allowed it to find another airport and land automatically, but the public and crews were not ready for it. On these test flights we flew from Teterboro on a triangular course to Westchester, then Floyd Bennett Field and back."

Back at Lockheed to complete their training, George and the other Australians would meet at the control tower cafe for morning coffee and doughnuts.

"On one occasion there, unbeknownst to us, Howard Hughes was sitting at another table with Paul Mantz, who was also very famous. He was known as 'the hydraulic king' and he was also a keen flyer. Anyway, Hughes heard us talking and came over to ask us where we were from. We told him and he introduced himself and we all shook hands. He was very affable."

Before leaving for home, George and some other Qantas staff drove down to Long Beach to see Hughes' most famous aircraft, the *Spruce Goose*, a

The L1049 Constellation, which arrived in 1952, was faster and had greater range and passenger capacity.

giant wooden flying boat designed to carry 1000 troops, which was flown only once, by Hughes himself. He had built an enormous hangar for the aircraft and they were given a guided tour because of their Lockheed connections.

"We were able to go inside the aircraft and I recall that the cabin dimensions were just astonishing, at least twice as wide as a modern Jumbo jet. We were used to flying boats which could carry 15 passengers, and here was this aircraft built to carry 1000 people."

During the eight months he was in the US, George was never able to phone home, but he wrote to Pam every week.

"Purchasing anything in Australia immediately after the war was very difficult, especially anything associated with apparel, so with every second letter, I sent her a pair of 15 denier stockings, which was a very fine nylon. I had learned to fold them in such a way that they got through without a customs charge on them."

George flew home in September 1947, with all the gifts he could carry. These included a pressure cooker, then virtually unknown in domestic kitchens and a vitrous enamel brooch of a maple leaf bought at Niagara Falls. For his boys, he posted back a huge Lionel train set given by friends in New Jersey and a small but sturdy two-wheel bicycle built by the Steerman Aircraft company. This bike is still in the family—George's new great grand-daughter, born early in 2000, is expected to learn to ride on it. Most astonishing of all, he brought back a black and white television set.

"Most people in the States didn't even have one yet and you couldn't get them here. A number of us brought one back and we had to convert them over in the workshops at Mascot, because Australia had a

George took this photograph of the Spruce Goose *at Long Beach, California in 1947 before its one and only flight.*

different number of viewing lines. We knew how to do that, because we had experts in electronics."

He also brought back the formula for a new industrial glue which Eclipse Pioneer had just developed. "This stuff took about an hour to mix in those days. Brian Murton and I were the first ones to bring Araldite to Australia."

George returned at a time of momentous changes within Qantas. In March 1947 the Australian government bought BOAC's shares in QEA, and in June, with the agreement of the Qantas board, the remaining Qantas shares, for £455,000. QEA was now a wholly government-owned airline. The old company, Queensland and Northern Territory Aerial Services, was wound up. Sir Fergus McMaster had retired as chairman earlier in the year, after years of failing health. Hudson Fysh was made chairman as well as Managing Director. After 26 years, he was now the top man.

Back in harness: George guides Ted White, a federal minister,
around the instrument overhaul section at Vickers Avenue, Mascot in 1948.
Jack Avery (centre), Qantas's first apprentice, looks on.

The first of four QEA Constellations arrived in October, a month after George's return. They began flying the London route on December 1, with QEA crews taking them all the way. The journey now took just under four days, and cost £585 return. For the first time, the passengers were tended by air hostesses, as well as stewards.

By 1950, QEA was expanding in all directions. They were flying Lancastrians to Japan, DC4s to Hong Kong, Manila and Malaya, Short Hythe-class flying boats to Singapore and Short S25 Sandringham-class flying boats to Fiji and Noumea. Catalinas operated to Lord Howe and Norfolk Island and in Papua and New Guinea, where QEA now flew an extensive route map with DH84 Dragons, DC3s and various smaller planes. The company no longer flew any Australian overland domestic routes. The old Queensland runs were taken over by Trans-Australia Airlines (TAA), a new government owned domestic operation. By 1955, QEA would also be flying scheduled services to Johannesburg via Mauritius, and Sydney to Vancouver via Honolulu and San Francisco, using the new 1049 Super Constellations, a bigger and more powerful aircraft that could carry 68 passengers. The company now had more than 5000 employees and was close to becoming a round-the-world airline.

Hudson Fysh received a knighthood in 1954 and gave up the day to day running in 1955. He remained chairman until 1965, but the new Chief Executive was Cedric Turner. Arthur Baird retired in 1949 and George was sad to see him go. This was the end of an era reaching right back to Palestine in World War I, when McGinness and Fysh flew Bristol Fighters and Arthur Baird fixed them.

Arthur Baird just before his retirement in 1949.

Baird died five years after retirement, in 1954. George believes that he would have preferred to keep working, had he a choice. "We had an extreme respect for him; respect for the work he had done in the past and his exceptional experience throughout the plant. When I joined the company, he knew his aircraft backwards. He always stood up for his team and he started the tradition of excellence in Qantas engineering."

Paul McGinness had a sad death, alone in Perth's Hollywood Hospital in 1952. He had reduced his age to enlist in the RAAF in WWII and was posted to New Guinea, but his old C.O. from WWI, now Air Marshal Richard Williams, saw him there and sent him back to a training job at Point Cook. After the war he failed at tobacco farming in Queensland and cattle export in the Northern Territory. He died of a heart attack and was buried in a Repatriation Department grave in Karrakatta Cemetery, Perth. Qantas later paid for a plaque honouring his role in founding the company.

That same year, George Roberts moved on from running the instruments overhaul section he had established 16 years earlier. He had no regrets.

"I became Engineering Equipment Officer and that meant developing or procuring all of the equipment which would handle the new aircraft on the ground."

There was a lot of work to do for the Super Connies, and by 1956 the Boeing 707 was on order, to arrive in 1959. This would be the next generation, as Qantas entered the jet age.

The new job was a promotion, but more than that, it was the kind of challenge he loved—solving technical problems by creative design and thought; building better mousetraps. He was part of the team that designed

and built new vehicles to tow the aircraft. They built the first luggage trains used at Mascot, because bigger aircraft meant more luggage. He oversaw the selection and installation of all new lathes and machining tools in the Repair and Overhaul Section.

He remains particularly proud of the motorised passenger stairs that he commissioned from Hastings Deering automotive engineers at Lidcombe. With hydraulics, the stairs could be raised or lowered to the doors of different aircraft. Mounting them on a specially designed chassis using Ford components made them fully transportable. They were also demountable to allow shipping on a DC3 or DC4, and fully roadworthy. In fact, when the first one was ready, George simply drove it from Lidcombe to Mascot, a big red and white staircase on wheels. All the major Australian airlines soon adopted the design, as did Pan Am, Air New Zealand and Malaysian Airways.

"When I became the Engineering Equipment Officer, one of the things I had to do was put forward applications to the Capital Expenditure Committee for various equipment we needed. It was headed by Scottie Allan. One of these was for a large petrol/electric crane. The crane we had at Mascot came from Rose Bay, for handling the engines on the flying boats, which were much smaller than the Constellation engines. It was a dangerous thing and totally inadequate. In fact, I used those words in one of my applications to the Committee, and the word came back that it was either adequate or it was not. Scottie Allan considered himself to be a student of the English language, you see. Anyway, I applied for five consecutive months to purchase the crane, which was going to cost £10,000, and each time it was knocked back. And so then I said to my people 'we've got to beat this fellow'."

George went to see the boss of Coles Cranes, suppliers of the new crane he wanted.

George's motorised stairs get a starring role, with the arrival in Melbourne
of Gregory Peck and his wife Veronique in 1959 for the filming of Stanley Kramer's
On the Beach.

"I understand that next month your crane is going up in price," George said. There was no response.

"I understand it's going up by a thousand pounds," George continued, "but providing I give you an order by the 24th of the month by 4 p.m., we'll get it for the old price, won't we?"

The Coles man agreed.

"You'll give me a quotation to that effect, won't you?' said George. More agreement.

This newfound bargain swayed the committee and George got his crane. Of course, the price rise was pure fiction.

"I thought, if I can't get it by the true means, I'll have to get it the other way, and it's still in operation today."

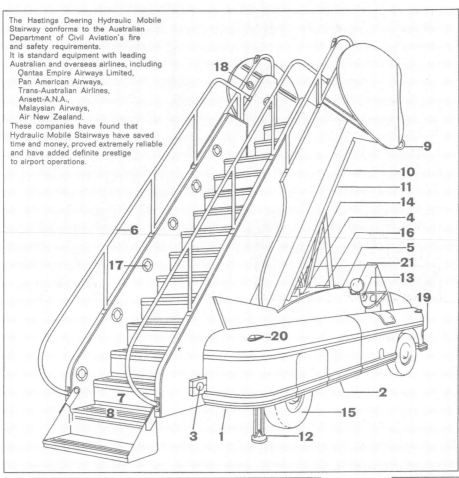

The Hastings Deering Hydraulic Mobile Stairway conforms to the Australian Department of Civil Aviation's fire and safety requirements.
It is standard equipment with leading Australian and overseas airlines, including
   Qantas Empire Airways Limited,
   Pan American Airways,
   Trans-Australian Airlines,
   Ansett-A.N.A.,
   Malaysian Airways,
   Air New Zealand.
These companies have found that Hydraulic Mobile Stairways have saved time and money, proved extremely reliable and have added definite prestige to airport operations.

1. Base chassis. 2. Housing for jack frame. 3. Housings for stairway frame. 4. Pump and reserve tank for hydraulic system. 5. 3 Driver's double-action control valves. 6. Stainless tubular steel handrail. 7. Steps of 10 gauge tubing and 14 gauge steel. 8. Anti-slip tread material. 9. 6" diameter tubular rubber platform bumper pads. 10. Hydraulic ram for elevating platform. 11. Jack frame of tubular steel, automatically locked from driver's seat. 12. Parking jacks, holding stairway firm for passengers. 13. Standard Ford controls for driver. 14. Fuel tank, 15 gallons. 15. Standard heavy duty car tyres. 16. Driver's seat, bucket type, Dunlopillo, Vynex covered. 17. Step lights. 18. Platform lights. 19. Head lamps. 20. Clearance lights to international airport requirements. 21. Spotlight for night manoeuvring. Full Specifications and Instruction Book available.

Hastings Deering Service Limited Manufacturers of Mobile Aircraft Stairways/Mobile Toilet Units/Mobile Water Units/ Tow Bars/Luggage Trolleys. Parramatta Road, Lidcombe, N.S.W., Australia. Phone 648 0111

Sole world-wide representatives
Qantas Empire Airways Limited, Head Office: Qantas House, 70 Hunter Street, Sydney, Australia. 'Phone 2 0369.

What the well-dressed team wore on the first Redex trial in 1953.
George and Don Roberts (seated) took part in all three Redex trials.

CHAPTER NINE

A Vintage and Veteran Man

George retired from Qantas in November 1970, after exactly 34 years with the company. He was then 60, at that time the compulsory retirement age for men. At his send off at head office in the city, the personnel manager, Verdon Sommerlad, told the assembled group, which included his wife and sons, that he had set a company record for attendance—not one sick day in 34 years.

They gave him a typically practical gift—"a mighty good electric drill, known as a Sher Trimatic, which is what I wanted". (Of course, he still has it and in the original box).

In the last six years with the company, he worked in the engineering property section, during a period of intense growth after the introduction of the Boeing 707. He was liaising with architects and contractors building new hangars for the jets, and supervising the equipping of new workshops.

"It was during this period that we developed the first hangar with a deluge system. That meant that in a fire, water could be dumped from the ceiling at the rate of 17 inches per hour (425 mm/hr). That was a huge amount of water, enough to extinguish a fire in a plane, but also save the hangar. The hangar was more important than the aeroplane in a way, because you can lease a new aeroplane tomorrow, but it takes some years to develop a hangar. It's not possible to take that amount of water from the mains, so we built a huge lake, which is under the stores section today. It's full of fish, living in total darkness."

In 1970, Qantas was preparing for the arrival of the Boeing 747 Jumbo. A week after he finished, he and Pam flew to Seattle to talk to the head of P.F. Industries Inc, a company which built specialised ground equipment for Boeing aircraft. George became the company's representative in Australasia.

"That came my way because in 1970, I was the co-director of the Australian Bicentenary International Rally for Veteran and Vintage cars, from Sydney to Melbourne, and the man who ran P.F. Industries, Dean Spencer, came out to drive in the rally. That's how I met him. He asked me if I would take on the job."

George spent the next two years organising sales and delivery of equipment such as tow-bars, jacks and lifting equipment for Jumbos to Qantas.

"It was quite a good business really but I had to give it away when Pam became ill. She meant more to me than the job."

Throughout the 1970s, Pam suffered from long and debilitating bouts of kidney and liver disease. "There was one year where she spent all but five weeks in hospital."

To pay the medical bills, George sold some of the vintage and veteran cars he had collected. When she was well, they would often go rallying together, which she loved to do.

"The last rally she went on with me took us out to Dubbo and Coonabarabran and all through the backblocks of western NSW. On the way back we lunched at Kurrajong Heights on the Bell's Line of Road, where a solicitor friend of ours took a photograph of her smiling in the car. Six weeks later she was gone."

She died on October 18, 1981, aged 71. "She said she thought she would never reach that age."

Pamela Roberts was cremated and her ashes interred at St Peter's Anglican Church, Watson's Bay, just over the hill from the home she and George had shared for 44 years.

Within a year he would also lose his younger brother Don, to bowel cancer. Don had stayed in Ipswich and resurrected the family car dealership after the war, making a success of the new Roberts Motors. He shared George's love of rallying and racing.

In the early 1950s, when there were fewer cars and no speed limits outside city limits, a Holden team set a speed record from Brisbane to Melbourne of 22 hours. "The Standard motor car people wanted to better that so they asked Don and me to have a go, so we did. We came down the New

England highway, driving through the night and we were in Parramatta in 10 hours. We were flying. We got to the GPO in Melbourne in 19 hours and 35 minutes. No stops, just straight through."

When the Redex trial started in 1953 the brothers decided to enter. This was a round-Australia endurance run designed to test both car and drivers. The rally was not just about speed. Drivers had to arrive at control points within one minute of the allotted time or they lost points.

"I introduced Don to it. I was a member of the Australian Sporting Car Club, which was organising it."

Contestants could use any car but there were strict rules about

Second Redex, 1954: Jack Jeffrey and George in their Volkswagen at Payne's Find, south of Meekathara in Western Australia. Trouble was awaiting them at Kalgoorlie.

replacing parts. "The cars were inspected and then sealed. Any part that could break or be replaced was painted with fluorescent paint, so that at the end of the trial they could check with infrared light to see if you had changed any parts. I know that one prominent team cheated, because Qantas carried 21 front ends up to Darwin for them. I knew about it because I was in Qantas. They knew what the paints were and had them all prepared beforehand."

In that first trial, George and Don drove a Standard Vanguard Spacemaster, fitted with extra fuel tanks to give them a range of 1000 miles. They finished eighth.

In the 1954 Redex trial, George and Don drove in different teams. The Volkswagen beetle was then new to Australia, and George was asked to co-drive and navigate for their first challenge. His new partner was Jack Jeffrey, with whom he had driven many club rallies in the previous eight years. These were often weekend "alpine trials" to the Snowy Mountains and back. "We used to bounce the car off snow banks going round bends in the winter."

Jeffrey was a crack driver but knew nothing about navigation. That was George's specialty, from his airline instrument work. "After we left Christmas Creek in the top of WA, we had to cross a salt pan which was 40 miles wide. We were the only ones who crossed it at night, because I used a compass and sextant to plot our position by the stars."

Some time later, approaching Broome, he realised Jeffrey was more tired than he looked. "He started calling me Sid. I told him he was troppo and took the wheel."

While Jeffrey was sleeping in Broome, George hired a taxi to reconnoitre ahead. He knew the roads were hard to distinguish, but he was dumbfounded at one of the road markers.

*Third Redex, 1955: George (left) reteamed with his brother Don
in the same Vanguard Spacemaster, the only car to complete all three Redex trials.*

"I told the cab to pull up when I saw an aircraft engine sitting beside the track. I said to the driver, 'that's a Pegasus X 'C' engine from an Empire flying boat'. He didn't know what I was going on about. It came from one of the flying boats wrecked in the Japanese raid on Broome, so it was probably an engine I had worked on."

He and Jeffrey lost no points until a faulty wheel hub stopped them at Kalgoorlie. They had to wait three days for a part, which disqualified them. Even so, they arrived in Sydney only 12 hours behind the winner, the famous 'Gelignite' Jack Murray.

In the third and final Redex trial, George teamed again with Don, in the same Standard Vanguard Spacemaster. The course covered 11,500 miles (18,500 kms) in 19 days, the vast majority of it on dirt roads. Again, they came unstuck on the Nullarbor Plain, when they ran into the back of another car.

"We had to average 70 mph across the Nullarbor, but someone had installed a road gate and grid near Eucla only three weeks before the run and after the rally survey had been done.

Third Redex: the Spacemaster, with its Nullarbor alterations,
still made it to the race finish at Parramatta Park.

"We were travelling in absolutely thick dust. We went over the grid and suddenly we saw the gate and realised the car ahead had stopped. Don was driving and he braked hard but there was no way we could pull up."

They ploughed into the back left hand side of the other car, pushing it through the gate, which had not yet been opened. The car stopped 50 feet further on, taking the gate and gate-post with it.

"The reason Don and I were saved is that we had installed aircraft seats in the car—a Catalina engineer's seat for the driver and a Liberator passenger seat for the navigator. We were wearing harness, not seat belts. The seat I was on had eight legs for extra strength, two on each corner, and all eight sheared off, but they just held on long enough to make me hit the windscreen and not go through it. I broke the rear vision mirror with my forehead and got a bad cut on my lip."

The car in front was a Plymouth, driven by Max Winkless, Peter Anthill and George Reid. None of them was injured but the Plymouth's left rear was well rearranged.

"I remember that Peter Anthill said to Don: 'If you wanted to put something in my bloody boot, why didn't you ask?'. And Don looked at him and said 'Peter, we did knock before we entered'."

The Plymouth finished the rally, but the Vanguard was extensively damaged. It took three days to effect some bush repairs, but they made it to the finish in Sydney, albeit disqualified. George and Don never attempted another round-Australia rally, although the trial continued for two more years with Ampol as sponsor.

"Three trials were enough. Very few people did all three Redex trials."

When Don died in 1981, George inherited a 1915 Model T Ford he owned. George still owns a 1927 T Ford, a 1903 Innes built by George Innes in Sydney, a 1912 Calthrope Minor, a 1921 Vauxhall and the 1909 FN motorcycle the doctor who delivered him rode to his birth. Over the years he has owned

Grand dames: George and Pam with the Calthrope Minor, known as Miss Prim, at the start of a 1959 Veteran Car Club of Australia (NSW) rally to the Blue Mountains.

and sold a 1914 T Ford, a 1908 Clement Bayard Tourer, a 1928 Delage DM Weyman Saloon, a 1923 Cadillac 'Doctor's Coupe', and a 1953 Mercedes 300B Saloon. For some years he drove to work at Mascot in a 1911 Rolls Royce Silver Ghost 'London-Edinburgh', owned by Jack Jeffrey.

"Of the cars I have owned, the Mercedes 300B was probably the best of all, but if you are looking for a vehicle which doesn't need much maintenance, the car I use today is a beauty. It's a 1967 Chrysler Valiant VC which I've owned for 12 years. One reason I like is that I can still do all of the maintenance myself. After that, the engines became much more specialised."

From 1978 to 1998, he was the Australian delegate to FIVA, the *Federation Internationale des Vehicles Anciennes,* which took him to rallies around the world. He remains an active member of the Veteran Car Club of Australia (NSW and Tasmania), the Vintage Vehicle Club of Australia, the Vintage Sports Car Club of Australia, the Rolls Royce Owners' Club, the Vintage Car Club of Great Britain, the Horseless Carriage Club of America and the Antique Automobile Club of America.

In car circles he is regarded as a world authority on the dating of old vehicles.

In 1985, four years a widower, George attended the annual general meeting of the Qantas Credit Union. At the supper afterwards, there was a shortage of chairs so he shared one with a woman he had known slightly at Qantas. Marie Heald had worked for Qantas for 24 years in the telecommunications section, retiring in 1976. She was a widow, her husband George having died in 1970.

"We got talking and a friend of hers came over and said she would give her a lift home and I said 'no you won't, I'll give her a lift'."

New lives: Marie Heald and George in Katoomba on the Veteran and Vintage Bicentennial World rally, March 1988.

George asked her out for a drive soon after. They picnicked at Commodore Heights, overlooking Pittwater. They've been together ever since.

None of George's brothers and sisters had children, but the Roberts line continues through George's two sons. Bruce, the elder, joined Qantas as an apprentice in engineering in 1963 and worked for the airline for 37 years, longer than either George or Norm. Bruce Roberts retired in 1998. Rodney trained as an automotive engineer, but he also worked for Qantas for 16 years. George's grandson James also worked for the airline for over 12 years. Between them, these Roberts men have logged 132 years at the airline.

George is the last surviving member of his family. Norm died in 1991, aged 83, from the effects of Parkinson's disease and glaucoma. Ivy never married, after her fiancée was killed flying in the battle of the Coral Sea. She lived on in the Ipswich home until her death in 1995, from leukaemia. She looked after their parents and worked as secretary at an Ipswich medical clinic for about 40 years. George's father died in 1964, his mother in 1978.

"The day I flew up to see her for the last time, Pam was just being released from hospital, so I was late getting to the airport. Norm got them to hold the aircraft for three minutes, so we could go together. I remember that night my mum said to me 'Well, I'm 89 years, four months and five days old and I won't be here in the morning', and she was right. She went during the night."

After Ivy died, George sold the family home at 7 York Street, East Ipswich, severing the last direct family link with that city.

Though he retired in 1970, George has never really left Qantas. Every Tuesday and Thursday, he rises early and drives the Valiant to Mascot where he works on the Qantas Historical Collection with other retired employees, answering queries from the public and within the airline.

His sense of history has always been acute, right from boyhood. He has never stopped collecting things, as various museums and the airline itself have discovered to their benefit. In the late 1990s Qantas apprentices in Sydney were given the task of restoring a Gipsy VI engine from the 1930s. George was able

Bert and Flo Roberts in the garden at 7 York Street East Ipswich, shortly before Bert died in 1964.

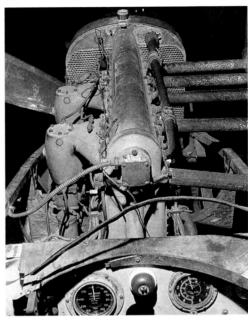

Sunbeam Dyak located near Lismore in the late 1960s.

to give them a number of original parts that he and Norm salvaged from the DH86 which crashed near Longreach in 1934 on its delivery flight to Qantas.

His involvement with preservation for the airline goes back to the late 1960s, when Hudson Shaw, who joined Qantas during the war, asked him to try to find a Sunbeam Dyak engine. This was the engine type used in the first Qantas plane, the Avro 504K built by Nigel Love at Mascot in 1920. In the late 1960s, the War Museum in Canberra loaned an intact 504K to Qantas, but it still had the original Clerget rotary engine.

"I wrote to various people around the country to see if anyone knew the whereabouts of a Dyak, and one of those was Bill Dousha, who was then chief engineer at East West Airlines in Tamworth. His brother George was one of the first engineers at Qantas. Bill came back to me with the registration letters of a 504K that had been there some years before and I traced that back

Engineer Bill Buttress-Grove test runs the RAAF Avro 504K, with the restored Sunbeam Dyak engine. The engine is now in the replica 504K housed in Qantas's domestic terminal at Mascot.

to Lismore. I had friends who ran the Ford dealership there and they gave me the name of a man who could guide me to the aircraft. It had been housed in a shed which had blown over and it was extensively damaged, but the engine and propeller were intact and a lot of the central section of the fuselage and the undercarriage. We brought it all back to Sydney and restored the engine and put it in this 504K from Canberra. The aircraft stayed with Qantas for the next 20 years, until the Museum recalled it, so then we had to switch the engines back again. Qantas then decided in the mid 1980s to build two complete full size replicas of the 504K. The major credit for that goes to Ross Woodcock and other retired Qantas engineers who were assisted by Qantas apprentices. I supplied some of the flying wires and turn-buckles and such, which we had left over from our own aeroplane-building days."

One of the two 504K replicas went to the Qantas Founders Outback Museum at Longreach, opened in 1996. The other is prominently displayed in the new Qantas domestic terminal at Mascot, with the Sunbeam Dyak engine and propeller from Lismore in its nose. Tantalisingly, when this replica was being installed in the terminal, a workman on the site told a Qantas official that he knew the whereabouts of the original Qantas 504K, registration G-AUBG. George knew that the aircraft was sold in 1926 to a Queensland aviation enthusiast called Frank Silverthorn, but what became of it was unknown.

"This fellow said it was in a barn outside Bundaberg. He didn't know the address, but he reckoned he could lead us to it."

Unfortunately, no one got the workman's name. George sought help from Tommy Quinn, who set up the Bert Hinkler museum in Bundaberg, but he couldn't find any leads, so the fate of the first Qantas 504K remains a mystery.

Only one pre-war Qantas aircraft is known to have survived. That's a DH80 Puss Moth, which Qantas flew from 1930 to 1932 in western Queensland and the Northern Territory. It was sold to Adelaide, and later bought by John Pettit, an aviation enthusiast from Wooloomanata Station, near Anakie in Victoria. George and Marie saw it under restoration when they went to the Avalon Air show in 1999. At time of writing (August 2000), the restoration was still underway.

The oldest surviving Qantas aircraft, the de Havilland DH80 Puss Moth, shown here in the early 1930s.

George Roberts is now the oldest living former Qantas employee and the only one left from the old Queensland days, before the company moved to Sydney in 1938. His career with the airline stretches from aeroplanes made with wood, wire and fabric to the Boeing Jumbo, from Gipsy Moths to behemoths. His love of aircraft goes back even further, to that first flight in a Curtiss flying boat when he was just 10 years old. He has forgotten very little and thrown away even less.

The oldest surviving Qantas employee, George Roberts.

Given his frequent brushes with deadly illness before the age of 21, his health since 1930 has been remarkable. "I've been exceptionally lucky in that respect, and I've been exceptionally lucky to have had the two girls I've had, both Pam and Marie. I consider myself very lucky to have two such wonderful mates."

His luck has held in another respect—his love of fast cars. He has now been driving for 83 years, having begun at age seven when he had trouble reaching the pedals. He still likes to drive cars fast, occasionally.

The usual words applied to people of his vintage are somewhat patronising: sprightly, well preserved, "all his marbles". They're also inadequate for someone like George, who concedes nothing to age. He's closer to indestructible. Like a Model T Ford, perhaps.

"I don't look upon tomorrow as being the end of the road," he says. "I look at what is ahead of me, what's still to do, irrespective of whether I will have time to do it."

Asked to sum up his own life, his answer is quick and chacteristically funny. "Very busy," he says, laughing. "It's never let up."

INDEX